CREATING
HISTORIC
SAMPLERS

Judith K. Grow

Elizabeth C. McGrail

CREATING HISTORIC SAMPLERS

The Pyne Press

PRINCETON

First edition
Library of Congress Card Number 74-78574
SBN 87861-069-3
Printed in the United States of America
Designed by Adrianne Onderdonk Dudden

CONTENTS

ACKNOWLEDGMENTS

We would like to express special thanks to Mary Ann Carkhuff, Lynda Pullen, and Gedske Szepsy, each of whom worked one of the new samplers included in this book.

We would also like to thank the many people who were generous with their time, their information, and their samplers: Laurenette S. Brewer of the Needle-Pointe, Pennington, N. J.; Joseph Franklin of Mayfair House, Inc., Lambertville, N. J.; Allan Grow; Christina Jackson, Philadelphia Museum of Art; Aviva Jacobs, The Jewish Museum, New York, N. Y.; Wendy Johnson of the Southport Gallery, Southport, Conn.; Zelda Kaman; Theodore H. Kapnek, Sr.; Priscilla Lord; Elsie S. McGarvey, Philadelphia Museum of Art; H. and R. Sandor, Inc., New Hope, Pa.; Ann Youngdahl Smith; Joan Toggitt, Ltd., New York, N. Y.; Barbara Ward, Essex Institute, Salem, Mass. Special thanks are also due to R. Joseph Restivo, Bob Sapienza and Mike Aronoff for color photography.

PREFACE

Interest in collecting American needlework samplers has increased greatly in the last ten years. Collectors, antiques dealers, and museum curators have stopped thinking of the sampler as a nostalgic curio and begun to consider it as a manifestation of the folk art of our ancestors. This serious interest in historic samplers has also aroused the desire of modern needleworkers to recreate them. In the last few years kits reproducing antique examples have become available, but there has been a dearth of patterns for the person who wants to do as her ancestors did—fashion her own sampler, using her own creativity to combine and adapt the traditional motifs.

An accompaniment to the popularity of collecting old needlework samplers is a growing interest in their manufacture and design. People ask, "When was it made? What kind of cloth is that? What stitches were used? What part of the country is that from?" The modern student or collector of the decorative arts wants to know these things because the sampler is not just something to be admired, but an artifact for understanding the past, a tool for investigating the social and cultural history of an earlier time. For the modern craftsworker, too, an understanding of the materials, the methods, and the traditions of the historical sampler is a necessary adjunct to creating modern adaptations of the older forms. An appreciation of historical American samplers provides a good background for the modern needleworker who wants to combine her own creativity with the use of traditional motifs.

The opportunities for study and research of early samplers are at once easier and more difficult than those in other areas of the decorative arts. Fortunately, great numbers of antique samplers have been preserved; they have survived in relatively greater numbers than many other artifacts of our past. The reasons for this are several. Families breaking up an old home were as likely to have kept an old sampler as any other object in the house—with the possible exception of silver or jewelry—because the family sampler or samplers could be accommodated in the smallest of modern houses or apartments. Since the sampler was a direct personal link with past generations, often signed with great-grandmother's name, it was much more likely to be kept than great-grandmother's redware pie plates, her iron cooking pots, or even her furniture. In other words, the highboy might go, but the sampler was almost certain to be passed down in the family. When samplers were disposed of, they were likely to be given to an historical institution rather than sold for what they would bring. The reasons were, and still are, sentimental. Families that did not cringe at the sale of other ancestral possessions were still not quite ready to put on the auction block samplers signed by their ancestors, so they often donated them, along with grandmother's wedding dress, to the local historical society or one of the state or national organizations for the preservation of relics. In the records of many such collections of samplers today, one finds over and over the notation "Sampler worked by the grandmother of the donor."

The comparatively low monetary value of samplers has also encouraged descendants to keep them or give them to historical societies. Fine silver or furniture is often worth so much on the open market that money outweighs sentiment, but until only recently even the finest samplers brought only a few hundred dollars. Even in recent years, when prices paid for antiques have grown by leaps, samplers—especially nineteenth-century examples—are still relatively inexpensive. All this—their relatively small size, sentimental family connections, and modest monetary value—helps to explain the preservation of so many samplers, both by the descendants of the original makers and in collections.

On the other hand, the fact that samplers were home- (or home-and-school) crafted items, rather than commercial products, has presented certain barriers to their study. When we want to study early manufactured items—the products of the potters or the cabinetmakers, for example— there are many tools available in the form of record books, account books, craftsmen's design books and the like. Samplers, however, present research problems because they were made by single individuals, rather than by craftsmen or artists who discovered or invented a successful design and then repeated its basic elements over and over. When we are able to study a number of works by a single folk painter, woodcarver, or fraktur artist, we can speak with assurance of that craftsman's "style" or "hand." Samplers, however, were made by girls or women who produced one or at most two samplers and then went on to other pursuits. Some samplers, especially those made at schools which used distinctive designs and motifs, are easier to categorize, but even here we cannot be entirely certain of their attribution because patterns and motifs were shared and motifs were carried from one school to another. Regional characteristics, however, frequently can be identified through the repeated appearance of characteristic motifs.

Another problem in studying early samplers—paradoxically, considering their number—is relative inaccessibility. Although many of the samplers that have been preserved are in institutions or collections, many are, as we have noted, still owned by descendants of the maker and are unknown to the researcher. And even many of those in museum collections are in storage and not easy of access. Another major complication arises from samplers within frames. Examining the underside of a table or of a pewter plate is one thing, but getting to the hind end of a framed sampler is another. In some ways the back of a sampler is even more informative than the front, because original colors and methods of stitching and finishing can only be studied from the back.

For all these reasons, the study of the sampler as a piece of decorative art has to some extent lagged behind the study of other antiques. Early researchers tended to concentrate on genealogical information about the worker and on the occurrence of various verses, rather than on designs, materials, and stitches. The genealogical study is, of course, important because it enables us to pin down with certainty the regional origin of samplers that do not include a place name, as most do not. Not enough attention, however, has been paid to questions of how samplers were planned and worked, to the materials used, and to the ways in which samplers were mounted and framed.

In this book we try to present information that will be of interest to both the collector of old samplers and to the modern embroiderer who wants to re-create her own version of the historical product. In so doing we view the sampler not just as an isolated example of the early needleworker's urge to decorate her walls or educate her daughters, but also as a manifestation of her social and cultural environment.

The new designs for complete samplers offered here are for the most part adaptations of existing old samplers, rather than exact copies. The designs for the individual motifs and alphabets, however, are as historically accurate as possible. Most are copied exactly from old samplers and are still workable in modern materials. The modern craftsworker who wants to create a new sampler can adapt these patterns to her own purposes, either replacing motifs on the sampler designs with her own choices or creating her own designs from the individual motifs and alphabets. We feel that many modern needleworkers do not want to reproduce exactly someone else's design. At least some of the impetus behind the modern craft revival stems from the desire of people to go back to the self-reliance of an earlier age, to design their own ornaments and products which they can then make themselves. The same turning away from mass-produced objects that has intensified the collecting of handmade antique furniture and pottery is evident in the modern interest in individualized, handcrafted needlework.

The collector of old samplers will, we hope, be interested in the techniques described for the creation of new ones because these techniques shed some light on the way old samplers were made. The modern needleworker will, on the other hand, have more appreciation of the form she is using if she better understands the historical tradition within which she is working.

CREATING
HISTORIC
SAMPLERS

1

ANTIQUE
AMERICAN SAMPLERS

A BRIEF HISTORY

The history of the American sampler begins in England and Holland. When the American colonies were first settled, a few of the women who made the voyage to the New World must have brought with them their precious samplers, or "examplars," or "samp-cloths." European women had been making samplers at least since the sixteenth century. These earliest samplers were true sample cloths since their owners used them to record stitches and patterns for needlework. In an age when paper was scarce and books were scarcer, the logical way for a woman to remember an interesting pattern or stitch was to copy it on her own sampler. Even a cursory examination of household inventories and account books of the sixteenth and seventeenth centuries will show that while cloth was bought and owned in relatively large amounts, paper was a very rare item indeed.

Very few early samplers have survived, so it is difficult to make generalizations about them, but they do have common design characteristics that distinguish them from later work. The most distinctive quality about samplers made prior to 1700 is their shape. They are all very long and narrow. The width varies between six and eight inches, while the length is anywhere from ten or fifteen inches to as long as three feet. Sometimes they were made of several pieces of cloth joined together, suggesting that when a cloth was filled, a new length was added to record more motifs. The samplers of the sixteenth century were almost always composed of scattered motifs, again suggesting that stitches and designs were copied as the embroiderer saw them. They seem to have been made by adult women, although in the sixteenth and seventeenth centuries a girl of fifteen or sixteen was considered an adult. It is tempting to guess that they were undertaken by a young woman about the same time that she began to take a serious interest in accumulating a dowry of household linen. Some early samplers show evidence of having been worked on by more than one person, so perhaps they were passed on and added to in the same way that handwritten recipe collections sometimes were. Perhaps they were even made by mothers as a present to daughters about to be married, given in the spirit that a modern mother might offer a copy of her favorite cookbook. Historians have indicated that these early samplers were rolled for storage, rather than framed and displayed. They were essentially working documents, not works of art. Indeed, when we look at one today, our admiration is usually for the exquisite neatness and interest of the embroidery, rather than for the artistic merit of the overall design.

By the seventeenth century the sampler had already begun to acquire some elements of convention and display, becoming a little more ordered than its predecessors. This progression may be seen in early samplers containing elaborate cut and drawn lacework patterns, copied probably from Italian lace-pattern books. In sixteenth-century samplers, these lace patterns are scattered throughout the work, indicating that they were copied at random. In seventeenth-century samplers, however, the lace patterns are often grouped at the bottom and the embroidery at the top, suggesting that the makers had a plan for a general design before they began. This may also mean that the embroidered part of the sampler was made first. The embroidery, though it was exacting and difficult, was not as demanding as the cut- and drawn-work designs. If this is true, as a few unfinished examples would suggest, the sampler had become by the seventeenth century a tool for the teaching of needlework, as well as a device for the recording of stitches and patterns.

The conventional nature of seventeenth-century samplers, both in America and England, is also suggested by their uniformly narrow shape —rarely more than nine-inches wide. This limitation was possibly imposed by the size of the fabric available, but, since most samplers of this period seem to be hemstitched on all four sides, the narrow width was much more likely a carryover from the sixteenth century when narrow samplers were used because they were easier to handle as well as to roll and store. The narrow shape is suited to the sampler that has a horizontal emphasis because each motif can occupy a single row. Since the designs on sixteenth- and seventeenth-century samplers were primarily border motifs for clothing and linen, the logical width for a sampler on which to record them is six to nine inches, a width that allows for one or two repeats of the bolder patterns.

These seventeenth-century traditions came to America with the earliest settlers. Several samplers in New England collections, made in England but brought to this country by the women who worked them, indicate that the sampler was considered precious and important enough to be carried to the New World. Indeed, they were particularly important because, in the wilderness that America then was, there would be found no other immediate sources of design. The Essex Institute in Salem, Massachusetts, owns one of these early imports, the sampler done by Anne Gower about 1616, presumably in England because she is thought to have emigrated to America only shortly before marrying Governor Endicott of Massachusetts sometime previous to 1628. A good example of the combination of drawn work and embroidery, this sampler, which is six inches wide and sixteen inches long, has its top half filled with embroidery and its bottom half with drawn work. Its vertical rectangular shape is typical of both English and American work of the period.

The earliest sampler known to have been made in America, worked by Loara Standish (a daughter of Miles) about 1640, is owned by Pilgrim Hall in Plymouth, Massachusetts. Of the same long rectangular shape, it is, however, all embroidery rather than a combination of embroidery and lacework. Because the size of the major horizontal cross-borders increases as the sampler goes on and a thin cross-border divides each of the major designs, the sampler presents a very ordered quality.

The sampler made by Mary Hollingsworth of Salem, Massachusetts, (fig. 1) is typical of the exquisite work of the period, insofar as a specimen of something so rare can be called typical. Though the sampler is undated, it was probably made about 1665 since Mary Hollingsworth was born in 1650 and married Philip English, a prosperous Salem merchant, in 1675. An excellent example of the horizontal emphasis of the seventeenth-century sampler, its motifs were embroidered in bands across the narrow cloth. These patterns were, at least according to tradition, the designs to be embroidered on household linen and wearing apparel. Indeed, the old label on this sampler reads, in part, "Patterns for Shawl Borders." The designs range from fairly simple and narrow cross-borders to the elaborate squared designs traditionally used for the corners of a shawl. That the sampler was planned, rather than embroidered at random, shows in the arrangement of the cross-borders. The large square design at the top balances the block at the bottom, and the motifs between the two are arranged in order of their width. As on other samplers of this period, small linear cross-borders separate and define the larger squared elements.

The stitchery of Mary Hollingsworth's sampler is to the modern eye extraordinary in its neatness. Each thread has been tied off in a tiny symmetrical knot rather than carried over to the next pattern, and the ends of the threads are worked into the pattern so that the back of the sampler presents evidence of the almost fanatical neatness of this seventeenth-century needleworker. The Mary Hollingsworth sampler, like others of the same period, was worked on a very fine linen cloth with what appears to be silk thread. The colors used are red, green, brown, and blue, the blue and green threads having retained much of their original color. The red, for the most part, has faded to a rosy brown, except in one segment of a flower border (the second from the top), where it has retained a vivid color. Either one batch of yarn had accidentally been made more fast than the rest—though this seems unlikely because the flower would have used only a short strand of silk—or perhaps some preservative, such as vinegar, had accidentally dropped on the sampler.

When the Colonial Dames published their pioneer survey *American Samplers,* in 1921, they recorded only seven American samplers of the seventeenth century, all but one from New England. That the geographic distribution was not wider is not suprising. It was primarily in New England that settlement was organized along the lines of the family-oriented village, with provision for education within the settlement. The Puritans' emphasis on education encouraged the cultivation of such didactic arts

Fig. 1.
Sampler by Mary Hollingsworth,
Salem, Massachusetts,
c. 1665. 25" x 7". Courtesy,
Essex Institute, Salem, Mass.

as sampler-making, and the village provided the opportunity for women to visit and to learn from one another. The permanent nature of the village was reflected in the creation of samplers, which, after all, implied that the maker expected to embroider other things later on. If seventeenth-century samplers from other parts of the American colonies exist, they will probably be found in those parts of Maryland or Virginia where towns were established early.

✖✖✖✖

Because there are so few of them, American samplers of the early eighteenth century are almost as difficult to discuss as those of the seventeenth. Of the nearly 1000 eighteenth-century samplers listed in *American Samplers* only fifty-three were worked before 1740, the demands of early colonial life apparently allowing very little time for fancy needlework. We can, nevertheless, draw some conclusions about the early eighteenth-century sampler. Presenting the transition between the long, narrow seventeenth-century example and the work of the late eighteenth century in which the format comes closer to the square, the pre-1740 American sampler was between six and twelve inches in width and was usually one and one-half to two times as long as it was wide. Still a reflection of the earlier "examplar," this shape was probably more a matter of custom than necessity for easy storage, since even early in the century samplers had begun to acquire the attributes of a decorative composition rather than being merely a collection of stitches. Narrow borders began to be used— first on three sides, then all around the sampler—a practice that continued until the borders often became more important than the sampler itself. Although the use of borders suggests that the sampler was now a totally planned and finished composition rather than a continuing record, the emphasis was still linear rather than pictorial.

The sampler done by Elizabeth Hudson in Philadelphia in 1737 (plate I) shows that the whole movement of this work is back and forth. The selection of borders was still the major pictorial effort of the sampler, indicating that these border designs were the chief concern of the embroiderer and that similar designs were probably used to ornament household linen and clothing. It is hard to be certain about this, however, because almost no ordinary household linen from the early eighteenth century has survived. Several other known examples of samplers done in the Philadelphia area in the 1730s suggest that this particular sampler is typical. But Elizabeth Hudson's work is especially unusual because it includes one of the earliest embroidered family records. Later in the eighteenth century and in the early nineteenth, the family-record sampler became common in America, but a family-record notation on a sampler this early is rare. Elizabeth Hudson's sampler was also a pioneer effort in that it includes a verse.

The shape of Elizabeth Hudson's work illustrates the transition from the long and narrow to the more square sampler of later years. It is eleven and one-quarter by fifteen inches, but the emphasis of the horizontal borders makes it look longer and narrower than it actually is. The horizontal borders are composed of square and triangular motifs in rows, an arrangement followed in the organization of the sampler as a whole. The top three motifs are based on a triangular design, making them appear to be quite narrow, while the bottom four rows, made up of alternating square designs, are much wider, again emphasizing the length of the sampler. The way that the family record and signature blocks are integrated into the blocks of the bottom rows of the border adds to the harmonious quality of the composition. The border of the sampler serves to tie the triangular and square designs together by setting a square flower inside a triangular line. This type of border, using a geometric flower inside an undulating line, was used as long as traditional samplers were made.

The irregularities in the design of Elizabeth Hudson's sampler—for example, the three square cross-borders are not perfectly centered; the petals of the flower in the third cross-border are not totally symmetrical; the outside border is not cornered exactly—are also typical of the layout and execution of the eighteenth-century sampler. Most of them are highly accomplished pieces of needlework done in tiny stitches on fine fabric, but the designs do not have the polish and precision of the seventeenth-century examples or the sometimes rather stiff symmetry of the nineteenth century.

✖✖✖✖

By the eighteenth century, the colonies were more diversified, both geographically and socially. The population of America was increasing rapidly—after 1700 the population of the British mainland colonies almost doubled every twenty-five years. As a result of this tremendous expansion, new settlements were pushed further and further away from the urban centers, and the individual farm, especially in the middle and southern colonies, was replacing the village as the center of life. At the same time, the settlers were further removed from their Old World roots. The result of all this expansion and diversification was that convention and tradition in such minor domestic arts as the sampler were increasingly replaced by innovation and invention.

As the eighteenth century progressed, the number of elements used on samplers widened tremendously. To the seventeehth-century concentration on border designs and perhaps an alphabet, the eightenteenth century added all the pictorial elements that we associate with sampler design today—Biblical scenes, farm views, schoolhouses, animals, trees, and many other motifs. The folk quality of these pictorial samplers is reinforced by certain minute awkwardnesses: off-center designs, imperfectly-cornered borders, and human figures larger than houses. That many of these designs had been used on other kinds of needlework and folk art in earlier ages only serves to emphasize that the sampler was becoming less and less a specialized form of needlework record and more and more another demonstration of technical skill.

The transition from needlework record to pictorial composition came about because the need for a catalogue of stitches decreased. Decorative needlework in the sixteenth and seventeenth centuries had been the pastime of the wealthy or of the noblewoman who had the leisure to decorate her household linen and clothing. Few seventeenth-century women anywhere enjoyed this favored social or economic status, but American women, no matter what their social status, probably had even less leisure than their European counterparts. By the eighteenth century, however, when many

Fig. 2.   *Sampler by Mary Ann Huntting, Dorchester, Massachusetts, dated 1880.*
Courtesy, Museum of Fine Arts, Boston.

American women had more leisure than their predecessors, printed books and patterns of needlework were more readily available, minimizing the need to record stitches on cloth. Because printed fabrics for bed coverings and curtains were also increasingly available, a woman who wanted colorful household textiles was no longer obliged to embroider them if she preferred to purchase printed cloth instead.

Not only were printed fabrics often substituted for embroidery, but surviving examples of American household linens suggest that the most common method of embroidered decoration was crewelwork executed in wool. Although the colonial housewife might be able to afford the luxury of silk threads when she wanted to embellish a purse or perhaps a waistcoat, she nearly always turned to wool when making such large articles as bedspreads or curtains, because wool thread was readily available from home-spinning and dyeing and the large-scale designs of crewelwork could cover cloth much faster than the intricate patterns found on early samplers. Preferring crewelwork, the American housewife no longer needed to start her daughters off in life with a record of the more delicate, more time-consuming, and more expensive silk-embroidery patterns.

Nevertheless, the practice of sampler-making continued, but the function of the sampler as a necessary compilation of stitches declined, replaced by the idea of its service as a record of achievement. Since fashionable crewelwork was pictorial in concept, the ability to create a sampler as a satisfactory composition became more important than the ability to execute intricate stitches. In fact, some of the motifs that found their way into the eighteenth-century sampler may have been adapted from the crewelwork of the period, for animals, birds, and naturalistic flowers were used on crewelwork embroideries before they began to appear on samplers.

About 1740, scenes began to appear on the American sampler. The earliest of these often take the form of a mound or hillock, with trees and flowers growing out of it, a motif which also shows up even earlier on crewel and needlepoint pictures. Frequently, especially in New England, a picture of Adam and Eve, usually standing on either side of the Tree of Knowledge, is the focal point of the scene. A number of samplers done in the 1740s in the Boston area show Adam and Eve and the Tree, with the Serpent coiled around it. Generally found at the bottom of these long, narrow samplers (usually about ten by seventeen inches), the Adam and Eve scene occupies about one-quarter of the work, the rest taken up by rows of cross-borders and alphabets. Several of these samplers are similar enough to indicate that they must have been done in the same school or under the direction of the same teacher. One of the prominent cross-borders on at least three of these samplers is identical to the cross-border on Mary Ann Huntting's sampler (fig. 2), worked in Dorchester, Massachusetts, in 1800. This duplication forms an interesting record both of the longevity of certain designs and of their regional character, since this border is rarely, if ever, seen on samplers from the middle states and the South.

In its initial stages the pictorial sampler included only a small scene, usually placed at the bottom of the composition. From the modest position of Adam and Eve in Massachusetts samplers of the 1740s, occupying only about one-quarter of the work's area, sampler scenes grew in prominence, becoming more and more true landscapes. On early nineteenth-century samplers, the scene often occupied most of the space, with perhaps only an alphabet and a border design testifying to the original form. This increasing prominence of the scene was one of the reasons that the sampler changed in shape and became more square. The long, rectangular shape was not really suited to the picture sampler in the same way that it was ideal for the alphabet and border samplers.

Like their American counterparts, English and Dutch samplers of the eighteenth century also incorporated much more pictorial material than had earlier examples. Distributing their pictorial work throughout the sampler rather than arranging it into a well-planned landscape, these European pieces were far less organized than even the simple designs of American samplers of the same period.

By the second half of the eighteenth century, additional types of sampler designs and new motifs had been developed. The stitching of a pious or sentimental verse became widespread, with many samplers given over completely to delicate, but boring embroidery of whole psalms or other Biblical verses. Even pictorial samplers often included a short Biblical verse or an adage. While many samplers continued to follow the pattern of a scene across the bottom and various cross-borders across the top, the latter, so prominent on the earlier works, were gradually minimized in importance and elaboration until later in the century they often were reduced to simple lines of stitches.

At the same time that cross-borders were declining in importance, an outside border was becoming more pronounced, acting as a frame for the composition and suggesting further the importance of the sampler as a pictorial composition. The borders were most frequently a stylized floral or fruit design repeated inside an undulating line, or a naturalistic floral design. Beginning in the 1760s in eastern Pennsylvania, for example, a unique design with a wide, stylized floral border was increasingly popular. The space defined by this border was divided into nine or twelve rectangles, outlined with simple borders. The rectangles were worked alternately in floral designs and verses, presenting the effect of a patchwork of small blocks held together by the wide border.

Samplers of the period in New England also utilized heavy frame motifs. As early as 1750, samplers of the same layout as Mary Richardson's (plate III) appeared with an elaborately embroidered border used as a frame for the central section. One, worked by Dorothy Lynde in Boston in 1757, has an elaborate border incorporating a figure of the sun at the top, cherubs in the corners, and a landscape with figures, a building, and animals. The central part of the sampler is a vertical rectangle, with alphabet, name, and numbers. The center was obviously considered less important than the border because its background cloth was left bare, unlike the completely stitched background of the border. Samplers like this were done in New England through the 1790s, at least one—dated 1766—(pictured on the cover of the June 1972 issue of *Antiques* magazine) using the format horizontally instead of vertically. In all these examples the border is more interesting than the rest of the sampler, and the central rectangle, with alphabet, verse, and signature, seems almost a concession to the sampler form.

The use of pastoral landscapes on eighteenth-century samplers is typical of the way in which American sampler design continued to diversify. Pastoral scenes had been used on needlepoint embroideries such as the "Fishing Lady" series in the 1740s, and, when they were introduced into sampler design ten years later, both the design idea itself and the samplers which employed it took on a vigorous new life. One of the most important elements to develop from the pastoral landscape was the representation of houses and other buildings. In the early landscapes, rustic houses were sometimes included as relatively minor motifs. Later, as the landscapes were simplified and the buildings became more prominent, the first fairly simple structures of the pastoral landscape gave way to an amazing variety —schoolhouses, public buildings, castles, churches, and even whole towns. The use of architecture as a sampler motif, a practice found in every sampler-making area of the country, ranged from the simple, small dwelling pictured by Mary Ann Lee (fig. 10) to the elaborate structures used by Abby Bishop (fig. 3) and Lydia Platt (fig. 9). There are some regional variations in the types of buildings and their treatment in the design. Girls of New England and New York State were more partial to sumptuous public buildings, while girls of the middle states, many in Quaker schools, were more likely to choose less elaborate buildings or private houses, a choice perhaps explained by the Friends' preference for plain design.

In addition to entire buildings, separate architectural elements, particularly columns and arches, found their way into sampler design. Columns in particular were used in all the sampler producing areas. The New Jersey family record shown in figure 8 is one of several from the northern section of that state utilizing very simple columns as a framing device for the record.

One of the most delightful of all architectural samplers is Abby Bishop's, dated 1796 (fig. 3). The elaborate building, a church or city hall, is framed by a columned arch with a banner suspended beneath it. Perhaps the columns and the arch represent the gates of heaven, for the sampler is a memorial to Abby's mother; the conventional mourning devices of weeping willows and urns, adapted no doubt from the silk-embroidered mourning pictures of the era, flank the columns and the building. The whole is framed with a free floral border which, with the interior frame of the columns, creates an interesting combination of two framing devices.

✖✖✖✖

In addition to the development of pictorial and architectural samplers, new sampler forms emerged in the second half of the eighteenth century. Darning samplers, appearing first in mid-century, continued to be worked for at least the next hundred years. In this form, holes were cut in the cloth and filled in with elaborate darning stitches. The effect is pleasing both because the patches were arranged symmetrically, often around a central medallion enclosing the name and date, and because the darning stitches were frequently worked in contrasting colors. In later nineteenth-century darning samplers, the stitches were sometimes worked directly over the cloth without cutting out a patch. Historically interesting, darning samplers are closer in conception to the original purpose of the sampler—a record of stitches—than most of the other samplers of the period. They are, moreover, particularly characteristic of the middle states, especially the area around Philadelphia, where they were often worked in Quaker schools.

Related to darning samplers and also associated with the Philadelphia
area in the last quarter of the eighteenth century are the Dresden and
Holliepoint samplers. These were, in a sense, a revival of the much earlier
cut- and drawn-work sampler. They were worked in white silk or linen thread
on fine linen or cotton fabric. The elements of the design were cut out of the
cloth and the holes filled in with needle-lace stitches, including a twisted buttonhole stitch known as Holliepoint. Jane Humphreys' sampler (fig. 4) shows
the most typical arrangement: a basket of flowers in the center, surrounded
by a border of squares and holes filled with the needle-lace. Sometimes the
central design was set off simply by a large openwork circle at each corner.

In contrast with the earlier cut- and drawn-work and openwork samplers, these illustrate perfectly the changing emphasis of sampler design over the course of the eighteenth century. Whereas the former were arranged as rows of patterns, these were clearly conceived of as pictures: compositions with carefully selected, balanced design elements.

✕✕✕✕

The increasing diversity of the sampler by 1770 was perhaps indicative of the prosperity and variety of the new land. By the third quarter of the eighteenth century, the eastern seaboard, where most samplers were worked, was no longer a wilderness. Boston, New York, and Philadelphia were small cities—not so sophisticated as London or Paris perhaps, but certainly not frontier settlements. Because there was a degree of comfort and prosperity even in the rural areas, young girls could be spared from essential household tasks so that they could be sent to school or taught fine needlework at home. Many schools and seminaries for young ladies were opened in all parts of the country, with needlework instruction an important element in the curriculum and the making of a sampler an important part

Fig. 4.   Sampler by Jane Humphreys, Philadelphia, dated 1771.
13" x 15". Philadelphia Museum of Art (gift of Miss Letitia A. Humphreys).

of that instruction. Sometimes schoolmistresses used the sampler as a device for learning not only stitchery, but other subjects as well. Samplers incorporating maps and even the multiplication tables were products of this dual educative function.

For some reason, map samplers, quite common in England, are rare in America. The stitchery on map samplers is usually of the simplest variety, commonly done primarily in outline stitch, often with the names of towns inked in instead of embroidered. The map was on occasion surrounded by a floral border, but this detail is uncommon. Among the most interesting American map samplers are those done at the Westtown School in Chester County, Pennsylvania. At Westtown in the early nineteenth century, some students embroidered actual covers for globes, rather than flat map samplers. A later map sampler, also of Pennsylvania origin (about 1840), is one of the few reflecting a needlework technique of any interest. This sampler, now in the collection of the Historical Society of Pennsylvania, features a map composed of needle-lace patterns, with a different pattern representing each county of Pennsylvania.

While the map sampler may have been a tool in the teaching of geography, the idea that the sampler in general was used in teaching the alphabet is a widespread misconception that calls for reexamination. Although it is true that great numbers of simple alphabet samplers were made by young girls, and equally true that many of the more elaborate samplers contained one or two alphabets, common sense tells us that the teaching of letters was not the primary purpose of these embroidered alphabets. Children in the eighteenth and early nineteenth centuries were expected to be able to read before they entered public schools at the age of six or seven. Consequently, they learned their letters early—sometimes, as in New England dame schools, as young as the age of three. Because most alphabet samplers were embroidered by girls of eight or nine, we can assume that these children already knew quite well how to read. Similarly older girls in their teens did not work alphabets on elaborate pictorial samplers to learn the alphabet, since a girl of twelve or thirteen who did not already know how to read was unlikely to be making a sampler at all.

A far more reasonable explanation for the existence of the alphabet sampler can be found in one of the practical functions of embroidery itself. A model for embroidered numbers and letters of the alphabet was an essential part of a young girl's education—someday she would be a housewife who would have to embroider identification marks on valuable household linen. All articles of personal clothing—as well as sheets, pillow covers, and towels—were carefully marked and numbered so that they could be counted and checked regularly. We can get some idea of how precious household linen was considered by looking at the care with which it was enumerated in old wills and household inventories; and we can get some idea of why it was so precious by reading a description of the labor that was necessary to produce a yard of linen cloth. The alphabet sampler, then, was an important teaching tool, but working it taught the embroidery of letters and numbers, rather than the reading and writing of them.

The importance of these alphabet samplers in the late eighteenth and early nineteenth centuries is demonstrated by their very number: they account for the greatest number of surviving examples by far. Although its very simplicity makes the alphabet sampler of this period far less memorable than more elaborate pictorial types, it has nonetheless a secure place in cultural history as the foundation of needlework training. Small in size and usually rectangular—sometimes longer than wide, other times wider than long—it contains little besides alphabets and numbers, the name of the embroiderer, and perhaps some simple motifs: a few flowers or birds, and plain linear cross-borders. The alphabet sampler did not really change with time; examples from 1740 are, in many cases, quite similar to those worked as late as 1830. Nor does it display the regional variations observable in more elaborate samplers, examples appearing remarkably similar from one end of the east coast to the other. The only exceptions are the distinctive Quaker samplers, which employ an alphabet not used in other areas. This alphabet, which may be seen in chart I, is distinguishable from alphabets used on other samplers because of its plainness. The serifs are squared, rather than curved, and the vertical elements have no decorative cross strokes, causing the letters to appear blocky and plain. The very timelessness and nonregional character of most alphabet samplers is evidence of their popularity and endurance as an educational tool.

In addition to fostering simple needlework such as the alphabet sampler, seminaries were responsible, too, for many of the elaborate and distinctive products of the era. Samplers from famous schools such as Miss Sarah Stivour's in Massachusetts and Miss Polly Balch's in Providence, Rhode Island, have always been sought by collectors for their intricate designs and because they can often be identified through their use of particular stitches, designs, or motifs.

Samplers worked at Miss Sarah Stivour's school make effective use of a crinkled, or raveled, silk, for depth and texture. The sampler done by Mary Richardson (plate III), which has been attributed to this school, gives a good indication of the richness that this silk produced when it was used as a background for a floral border and landscape. At Miss Stivour's school, crinkly silk in long, irregular triangles was placed at the top and bottom of the sampler to represent the sky and grass, a technique so closely associated with the school that it is called Stivour stitch by modern collectors. Samplers with Stivour-stitch triangles were invariably organized like Mary Richardson's, with a landscape at the bottom, a floral border, and a central rectangle containing the signature block with a verse or alphabet. Although the exact location of the school is unknown, it is presumed to have been in the area of Salem, Massachusetts, because many of the samplers associated with the school have been found there, and several of the girls who signed typical Stivour's-school samplers are known to have lived in Salem. The school is thought to have been in operation between 1778 and 1786.

Equally famous are samplers done at Miss Polly Balch's school in Providence, Rhode Island. These combine architectural motifs with landscape and other decorative motifs to achieve some of the most elaborate effects ever found in American samplers. They are unusual in that the entire ground of the cloth is covered with stitches, giving a very rich tapestry-like effect to the completed works. The central design is usually a house or a public building in a fairly intricate landscape, framed by elaborately figured columns stitched in such a way that they appear to be raised and textured. In the sampler done by Lydia Gladding in 1796 (plate II), the technique can be seen clearly in the columns. Though the stitchery is very simple, the alternating bands of color produce a spiral, rounded effect, not unlike the optical illusion of a barber pole. The floral border around the outside of the sampler adds to the richness of the effect because it is done in rococo stitch, which has a raised, textured quality. Some samplers from Miss Balch's school feature large flowers in rococo stitch at each corner of the scene, rather than the border shown in the Gladding example. The samplers worked at this school, combining intricate designs and rich texture in a small space (Lydia Gladding's sampler is only twelve by twelve inches), are among America's most sophisticated.

Elaborate, distinctive samplers also were worked at schools in Pennsylvania. In the late eighteenth and early nineteenth centuries, several schools in the Lancaster-Harrisburg area turned out the finest of pictorial work. These, principally from Leah Galligher's school in Lancaster, Leah Meguir's school in Harrisburg, and Mrs. Welchan's in Maytown, feature a border divided into squares. Each square contains a heavily embroidered motif—hearts, flowers, butterflies, geometrics, and so forth. The central section displays either a finely embroidered scene or an inscription. These samplers were often worked on a fine linen or muslin gauze known as "Tiffany Gauze" or "Hankerchief Linen." The figures, and sometimes the other motifs, are accented with beads, sequins, and metallic threads, the use of which is uncommon in American samplers. Sometimes in these Pennsylvania samplers delicate features, such as faces and arms, were painted directly on the linen. This technique was probably adapted from silk-embroidered mourning pictures, in which parts of human figures and inscriptions on funerary urns were often painted directly on the silk. In sampler design, these elements were sometimes painted on paper which was then fixed to the linen.

Less elaborate, but equally distinctive, are the Quaker samplers made by girls in the various schools established by the Society of Friends. The most famous, and oldest, of these Quaker schools was the Westtown Boarding School, opened by the Philadelphia Yearly Meeting of the Society of Friends in Westtown Township, Chester County, Pennsylvania, in 1799. The simplest Westtown School samplers consist of an oval border of vines and leaves, framing the distinctive Westtown alphabet (see chart I) and a few simple geometric motifs. This alphabet is the hallmark of Quaker samplers and was used in schools at Pleasant Hill and Fallsington, Pennsylvania; the Westfield School in New Jersey; and the school operated by the Yearly Meeting of the Society of Friends of the State of New York, known as the "Nine Partners Boarding School," in New York City. A number of darning samplers from these Quaker schools have survived, as well as a few slightly more elaborate ones, including one stitched in 1809 by Martha Heuling of Moorestown, New Jersey, which contains a picture of the school. No matter what their form, samplers from Quaker schools are invariably simple and subdued. This simplicity is perhaps more appealing to modern eyes than the rich colors and stitchery of more elaborate and intricate samplers.

One of the most fascinating aspects of the design of late eighteenth- and early nineteenth-century samplers is the spread of design elements, stitches, and motifs from one school to another. That samplers made in

Quaker schools are uniformly simple is to be expected; that many have identical motifs and alphabets indicates the spread and migration of design through the agency of graduates of those schools. The Westtown School, for example, drew students, male and female, from the whole area under the direction of the Philadelphia Yearly Meeting. Since girls, as well as boys, were expected to make some use of their education—particularly through teaching—graduates of Westtown School went on to teach in other places, spreading the distinctive sampler designs used there. For example, the pupils at the Pleasant Hill School, founded by two Westtown graduates, made samplers almost identical with those produced at the older school.

A motif which evidently also was transmitted through schools within a particular geographical area is the "Emblem of Love" design. This is a simple octagon, with two pairs of love birds and the words "An Emblem of Love," or sometimes "A Token of Love," or "An Emblem of Innocence" (see chart XIX). This motif was used widely on samplers done in schools in the Philadelphia area and in nearby Chester County. It also appears on samplers worked in Trenton, New Jersey, including one signed "Worked by Jane Sutterley at Miss C. Redman's Seminary in the 8th year of her age . . . July 4th A. D. 1839."

The repetition of favored design elements in other regions suggests some like manner of communication among needleworkers. For example, the distinctive layout and stitchery of samplers associated with Miss Stivour's school is not confined to work done at that institution. Samplers with the same general layout were made as early as 1750, over a quarter of a century before the school is thought to have opened. The technique of long satin stitches done with a crinkled thread, as well as the rural landscape with figures, continued to be used in New England samplers after Miss Stivour's school had probably closed. For example, Mary Ann Huntting's sampler, dated 1800 (fig. 2), features a broad cross-border of the crinkled satin stitch, as well as a landscape which is very similar in concept and layout to those on the Stivour's-school samplers. However we can be reasonably sure that Mary Ann Huntting did not work her sampler at Miss Stivour's both because its date is later than the generally-accepted date of the school's termination and because its present owner, the Boston Museum of Fine Arts, also owns an elaborate needlework picture done by her at Miss Beache's Academy in Dorchester, Massachusetts. Even when samplers combine all the characteristics usually associated with the school, it would probably be more accurate to state that there was a preference for these motifs and techniques in Salem and other areas around Boston than to attribute such pieces to Miss Stivour's.

These few examples of the transmittal of motifs, designs, and techniques in several areas of the country serve as a reminder that the people of early America were not necessarily isolated and untraveled. They should also prompt caution in the attribution of samplers, or other forms of decorative art, within too narrow an area. Such urban centers as Boston and Philadelphia exerted a design influence over a rather wide hinterland. For samplers, this is particularly true after the formation of young ladies' seminaries and boarding schools. Girls went to school many miles from home, returned, and taught their own children or pupils the stitches and designs they had learned in school.

However, it must also be remembered that the famous schools such as Miss Stivour's and Miss Balch's account for only a fraction of the samplers done in the last quarter of the eighteenth century and the early part of the nineteenth. Probably, however, most of the elaborate examples like Abby Bishop's (fig. 3), Mary Wiggin's (plate IV), and Jane Humphreys' (fig. 4) were worked in fashionable seminaries, even though we can not presently identify the schools in which these samplers were made.

Unlike such simple forms as the alphabet sampler, in which traditional designs persisted over a long period of time, pictorial samplers reflect changing fashions and tastes. Mary Wiggin's sampler, dated 1797, illustrates the American pictorial sampler in transition from the eighteenth to the nineteenth century. The border of the sampler is small in proportion to its overall size, but its importance as a framing device is greatly heightened by the use of color. The shape of the sampler is no longer oblong, but it is not yet square. Measuring eighteen inches by twenty-one and one-half, it seems even more horizontal than it is because of the way in which the design is arranged. The elements of the two cross-borders, with their squared and triangular designs, are reminiscent of some of the borders on much earlier samplers. The organization of the landscape at the bottom is a delightful combination of eighteenth-century crewelwork mound design and the much more stylized work of the Federal period. The landscape is totally symmetrical, lines dividing the basket of flowers from the more naturalistic trees on either side, providing a frame and emphasizing the highly organized quality of the whole. Mary Wiggin's sampler, like those done at Miss Polly Balch's school in Providence, is unusual in that it is embroidered all over, although it differs in many other ways from the samplers done in Miss Balch's school. The latter have the effect of tapestry because of their quite sophisticated color choices, their shading, and their very intricately composed landscapes. On the other hand, Mary Wiggin's sampler is more like folk painting in its use of large blocks of striking color and the boldness of its design.

✕✕✕✕

Pictorial samplers of the period from 1800 to 1840 are often almost square or of a subtly rectangular shape. The samplers range in size from about sixteen to twenty-four inches square, with the rectangular shapes employing about the same area. Samplers from this period almost always display a prominent border, usually on all four sides, although some examples have a landscape at the bottom and the borders on only three sides. The borders are either floral or geometric and usually are worked in cross or satin stitch. They frame a strong, well-organized design, emphasizing the idea that the sampler is a picture, continuing a characteristic that first appeared in the 1760s.

The designs of early nineteenth-century samplers are dominated by animals, buildings, and floral arrangements. The buildings and floral patterns are often more elaborate than the work of the eighteenth century, but the animals have, in many examples, become less interesting. Though horses, sheep, and even wild animals like lions appear, the bird and the dog are the most common. The birds are generally less elaborate than eighteenth-century examples worked with real imagination, like those pictured in rather improbable flight on the bottom of Mary Richardson's sampler (plate III). In the nineteenth century these are replaced by simple, stylized, profile figures. The flowers and trees on nineteenth-century samplers, in contrast, are frequently more naturalistic and sweeping than the stylized flowers in the borders of many early samplers. The popularity in nineteenth-century needlework of the weeping willow, with its drooping, sweeping lines, attests to the taste for the botanically naturalistic which stands in surprising opposition to the rigid animal forms of the same period.

In spite of the natural quality of some of the early nineteenth-century foliage and flowers and of the variety of the buildings and other motifs of this period, an increasing stiffness becomes apparent and is intensified in the years following the late 1820s. Although the sampler becomes increasingly rigid, it lacks the precise stitchery of the earlier stylized examples of the seventeenth and eighteenth centuries. Characteristically the human figure is very rarely depicted on American samplers made after 1810; pastoral ladies and gentlemen are almost totally absent and even Adam and Eve rarely occur, although they are still a popular motif on English samplers of the period. Mary Ann Huntting's sampler (fig. 2) combines some nineteenth-century characteristics with some of the designs of the earlier period: the pastoral landscape, the crinkled-satin stitch, and even a border that can be found as early as 1740. Comparison of Mary Ann's landscape with the landscape on Mary Richardson's 1783 sampler shows how the figures have become stiffer. Compare the ladies presenting bouquets of flowers to gentlemen at the bottoms of the two samplers. The earlier female figure, though not well-proportioned, has a roundness and detail lacking in the 1800 sampler. Even the lines of the two men's coats show how much more spontaneity there was in the delineation of the human figure in the earlier sampler.

The sampler made by Rachel Ann Herring in New York in 1827 (fig. 5) is a good example of early nineteenth-century work at its finest. The naturalistic border on all three sides and the prominent landscape at the bottom provide all the interest. Though the alphabet and signature occupy as much space as the landscape, their impact is minimal. The combination of the naturalistic border and the romantic landscape is typical of the early nineteenth century. Sky and water and sailboat are almost impressionistic —the water and sky seem to be in motion because of the lines of the stitches. Opposed to this is the whimsical quality of the turreted castle. This seascape is, incidentally, an extremely rare design for American samplers. Only a few other examples with pictures of ships are known.

The early nineteenth-century Adam and Eve sampler (fig. 6) combines the same sense of unreality and naturalism. Even though the border is minimal in stitchery, its impact on the organization is clear. The verse at the top of the sampler seems to be almost an afterthought. The real force of the sampler is in the figures of Adam and Eve dominating the landscape and in the improbably floating baskets of flowers. Indeed, the baskets serve to frame Adam and Eve, rather than to distract attention from them. The strange castles, with birds instead of flags perched on the flagpoles, also seem to move Adam and Eve further into the foreground because they add an optical illusion of perspective to the sampler. Adam and Eve are stitched in light-colored satin stitch in such a way that they seem almost alive.

Fig. 5.   Sampler by Rachel Ann Herring,
New York, dated 1827.
17¼" x 17". Philadelphia Museum of Art:
The Whitman Sampler Collection
(gift of Pet, Incorporated).

Fig. 6.   Sampler, American,
early nineteenth century. 17¼" x 15¼".
Philadelphia Museum of Art:
The Whitman Sampler Collection
(gift of Pet, Incorporated).

Fig. 7.   Sampler by Sarah G. Tate, Pennsylvania, dated 1809. 20" x 17".
Philadelphia Museum of Art:
The Whitman Sampler Collection (gift of Pet, Incorporated).

Sarah Tate's sampler, made in Philadelphia in 1809 (fig. 7), empha-
sizes the border even more heavily than most nineteenth-century pieces.
The whole vitality of the sampler is in the border, rather like some of the
New England samplers of the mid-eighteenth century. The border is composed in an organic fashion, with the vines and flowers growing out of the
cornucopiae at the bottom. Sarah Tate's sampler is unusual in that it is
stitched on green linen rather than on the creamy tan color used for most
American samplers. This green linen canvas was used occasionally for
samplers from the 1780s until the first quarter of the nineteenth century.
Although its use is uncommon, examples of it have been recorded from
Pennsylvania, Massachusetts, Vermont, and New Hampshire.

✖ *CREATING HISTORIC SAMPLERS* ✖

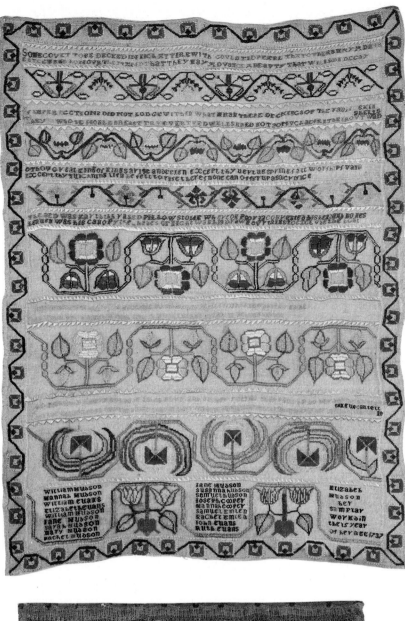

Pl. I.   *Sampler by Elizabeth Hudson,*
Philadelphia, dated 1737.
15½″ x 11¼″. Philadelphia Museum of Art:
The Robert L. McNeil, Jr., Trust Gift.

Pl. II.   *Sampler by Lydia Gladding,*
Providence, Rhode Island,
worked at Miss Polly Balch's school, dated 1796.
12″ x 12″. Private Collection.

Pl. III.   *Sampler by Mary Richardson, Salem, Massachusetts,*
possibly worked at Miss Sarah Stivour's school,
dated 1783. 20" x 20½". Courtesy of Essex Institute,
Salem, Massachusetts.

Pl. IV. *Sampler by Mary Wiggin, American, dated 1797.*
18" x 21½". Philadelphia Museum of Art:
The Whitman Sampler Collection (gift of Pet, Incorporated).

Decend sweet hope thou soothing power
From whom the weary find
In every dark afflictive hour
Some solace to the mind.

Alice Maris's Work.
Marple

Pl. V.   Sampler by Alice Maris,
Marple, Pennsylvania, c. 1814.
21½" x 21".
Philadelphia Museum of Art:
The Whitman Sampler Collection
(gift of Pet, Incorporated).

Pl. VI.   Sampler by Elizabeth Leeds,
Cumberland County, New Jersey,
dated 1846. 25½" x 25".
David and Elizabeth McGrail.

One of the most popular types of samplers made in the early nineteenth century was the family-record sampler. Although family-record notations were made on American samplers as early as the 1730s, the sampler which used this record as its central feature is largely a product of the period from 1800 to 1840. Family records painted in watercolors on paper were popular at the same time, indicating that samplers probably shared common design sources with other folk art forms. Record samplers occur in many styles, the most common being the list or table centered and surrounded by either a floral border or architectural motifs. Elizabeth Avery's sampler (fig. 8), done in 1829, in Montville (probably New Jersey), illustrates the layout of the simplest type—the genealogical table flanked by simple columns. As in Elizabeth Avery's example, deaths were often recorded in black thread, while colored thread was used for births and marriages. Elizabeth Avery's sampler is unusual because it records more than two generations, most family records listing only the parents and siblings

Fig. 8.   Sampler by Elizabeth M. Avery, Montville, probably New Jersey,
dated 1829. 18½" x 18". Philadelphia Museum of Art:
The Whitman Sampler Collection (gift of Pet, Incorporated).

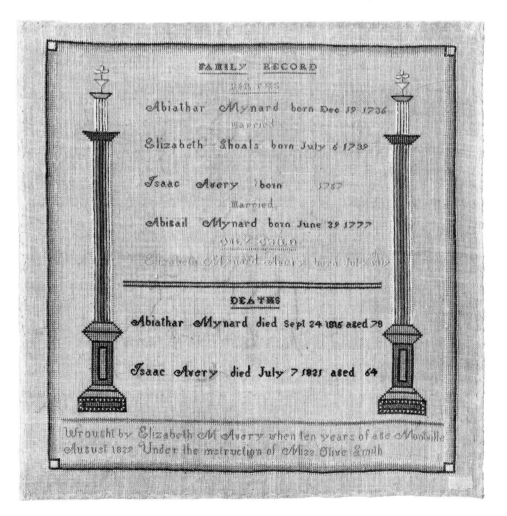

of the embroiderer. More common than the architectural border on family-record samplers is a freely-embroidered satin-stitch floral border or a geometric border, usually worked on all four sides. The family record was frequently combined with other motifs—a series of alphabets, a floral arrangement, or more rarely, a landscape. Occasionally the family record takes the form of a tree, with names recorded on the branches or fruit, but this type is quite rare. Family-record samplers from other countries are also rare, the form apparently being a particularly American tradition.

An equally popular form in the early nineteenth century was the so-called "schoolhouse" sampler. Buildings had of course been used on samplers over a long period, imposing architectural forms having dominated many works of the last quarter of the eighteenth century. By the early nineteenth century many samplers featured a single dramatic building, sometimes standing alone, sometimes as part of a landscape. These examples have come to be called schoolhouse samplers by modern collectors because many of them have been thought to represent the school building where the sampler was worked. The houses range from simple structures filled in cross-stitch to elaborate ones where every brick is outlined in a contrasting color. As befits a schoolhouse, the building is often stitched in red.

The schoolhouse sampler included among the new designs in this book (plate IX) is based quite closely on an old example done by Mary Fowser in Salem County, New Jersey, about 1840. The large red building, which is perhaps a picture of the Quinton, New Jersey, school, is embroidered in tent stitch with red wool. The entire design of the sampler is dominated by the schoolhouse, with the fences and trees acting simply as adjuncts to the houses.

Lydia Platt's marvelous representation of Solomon's Temple, done in 1850 (fig. 9), is an indication of how long the schoolhouse sampler continued in vogue. Though Lydia Platt's work is not, in the strictest sense of the word, a schoolhouse sampler since the building pictured is Solomon's Temple, her work demonstrates how the idea of the sampler featuring a single, dominant building was reinterpreted over and over. Solomon's Temple is, in fact, a design that had occurred earlier than on Lydia Platt's work. Two representations of the Temple, one on an American sampler from 1820 and another on an English sampler from 1829, both feature the same turreted, many-windowed edifice used by Lydia Platt.

Alice Maris' design of a house perched at the top of a green lawn with white animals (plate V) illustrates an interesting regional variation of the early nineteenth-century house sampler in the Philadelphia area. Rare examples of this type of sampler have an American eagle in the sky above the house, one of the few known uses of this popular motif in early republican samplers. Alice Maris' sampler is crowded with various motifs—the house, the floral arrangements, the butterflies, and the signature block—but it is not unpleasantly busy. The blocks of solid color at the bottom of the sampler—the green lawn and the white animals—balance the elaborately embroidered sky and the floral border.

Examples of this "house on a green lawn" design were probably not the product of a single school, although they were all made in the Philadelphia area. Alice Maris' sampler was made in Marple, Pennsylvania; another with a similar format, done in 1801 and signed "Wrought in Burlington"

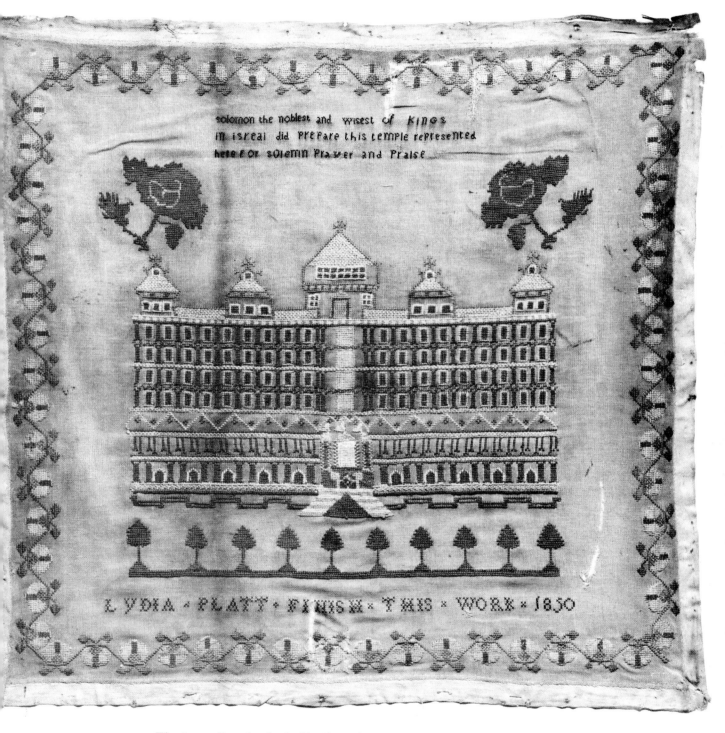

Fig. 9.   Sampler by Lydia Platt, American, dated 1850. 24″ x 26″.
Philadelphia Museum of Art: The Whitman Sampler Collection (gift
of Pet, Incorporated).

is apparently from Burlington, New Jersey. A third, done by Eliza F. Budd in 1808, is presumably a view of the Courthouse at Mount Holly, New Jersey.

Mary Ann Lee's sampler, done in 1826 in Richmond, Virginia, (fig. 10) is not, strictly speaking, a schoolhouse sampler because the house does not occupy a prominent place in the design. It is, however, another indication of the manner in which houses continued to be used as a motif on

Fig. 10.   *Sampler by Mary Ann Lee, Richmond, Virginia, dated 1826. 18″ x 19½″. Courtesy of The New-York Historical Society, New York City.*

American samplers. In this case, a small, simple dwelling is linked with neoclassical urns and weeping willow trees. The layout of Mary Ann Lee's sampler is unusual: it is divided into two narrow horizontal rectangles, both embroidered in pictorial motifs. On nineteenth-century samplers, it is much more common to find the signature strip at either the top or the bottom. Sometimes there is an alphabet at the top, the signature strip below this, and then the pictorial element at the bottom, but in this case the alphabet and signature are almost always outweighed by the impact of the scene at the bottom. In Mary Ann Huntting's sampler (fig. 2), for example, the verse, alphabet, and signature strip occupy as much space as the landscape, but they are reduced in importance by the dramatic blocks of color and stitchery of the landscape. The center strip on Mary Ann Lee's sampler, on the other hand, has the effect of making a nearly square sampler (eighteen by nineteen inches) into two rectangles, each with its own design.

✖✖✖

Samplers made by Pennsylvania-German girls bear little resemblance to the pictorial samplers popular elsewhere in the country in the early nineteenth century. These Pennsylvania-German products are distinctive folk pieces entirely different from the carefully landscaped houses, or the alphabet and family-record samplers.

The sampler by Susana Landis (fig. 11) is typical of the products of the Dutch Country. Though the motifs are very symmetrical, they are scattered throughout the sampler, rather than arranged in a consistent landscape. The pattern is orderly and balanced, but shows none of the pictorial quality of samplers from other areas. The long-tailed peacocks facing one another are popular on Pennsylvania-German samplers, as are the pair of deer, seen in this example in the lower left-hand corner. The six-pointed symmetrical star is also a popular motif. The scattered initials are characteristic, recording the maker's parents and siblings, although Susana Landis also recorded her parents' full names across the top of her work. Alphabets and verses are used occasionally on these Pennsylvania-German samplers, but rarely occupy the place of prominence accorded them in other sampler-producing regions.

The motifs on Pennsylvania-German samplers are usually angular. The heart in the center of Susana Landis' work is a fine example, its sides and top straight lines rather than curves. Even the tulips and carnations on such samplers are often made up of angular sections. In fact, very little free embroidery of satin or stem stitch, appropriate to rendering curved lines, was used on Pennsylvania-German samplers. Instead, these pieces were often worked entirely in cross stitch, contributing further to the angularity of design so characteristic of their type.

Pennsylvania-German samplers like Susana Landis' were often made without the border typical of other nineteenth-century pieces. If there is a stitched border, it is often quite spread out and minimal in impact. Rarely is it defined by a line of stitching to set it off from the rest of the sampler. The stitched border, however, is frequently replaced by a binding of silk ribbon. These ribbon borders, used all through eastern Pennsylvania and occasionally in New Jersey, were handled in two ways. The ribbon

One example in the collection of the Jewish Museum, made by Rachael I. Seixas in New York City about 1830, is silk embroidery on linen with a floral border enclosing a verse, precisely in the tradition of the early nine-teenth-century American sampler. Indeed, unless a sampler has a reliable family history, or unless we are able to identify it through the presence of a Hebrew alphabet or other ethnic design motifs of particular religious significance, we have no positive way of identifying a Jewish-American sampler.

The same problems of identification occur with samplers worked by black girls. Since Quaker meetings in the Delaware Valley were providing for the education of black children as well as white as early as 1770, we can assume that at least a few Quaker samplers were worked by blacks. In the absence of reliable family history or of other concrete documentation, however, there is no way to differentiate between the samplers made in Quaker schools by black girls and by white girls.

✖✖✖

After the period from 1840 to 1850, the American sampler began to decline in inventiveness. The importation of Berlin patterns from Germany, beginning about 1820, did much to discourage the spontaneous quality of American needlework. Berlin patterns were exact stitch-graphs, suitable for working in either wools or silk on a fairly coarse canvas. The charts were handpainted square by square, and many were adapted from prints which called for a great deal of shading in the designs. This very careful shading, of course, succeeded in eliminating the blocks of color that give such vigor to some of the earlier products. In previous periods strawberries and occasional flowers had been shaded, but seldom in more than two colors. Berlin patterns introduced shading of three or more tones, and also introduced a sense of perspective to the designs, eliminating the flat quality that characterizes so much folk art.

Berlin patterns did not replace the individually-designed sampler overnight, and many traditional samplers continued to be made into the 1840s, but more and more elements from the patterns became evident in sampler design. By the 1840s Berlin patterns were available not only in shops, but in ladies' magazines, and their widespread distribution made certain that much that was individual and regional in the character of American needlework would eventually disappear.

Sometimes the Berlin patterns were combined with traditional sampler designs to produce effects like those of Elizabeth Leeds' sampler (plate VI), done in Cumberland County, New Jersey, in 1846. The border pattern and the central motif were almost certainly taken from a Berlin pattern and look remarkably like a modern needlework design. Elizabeth Leeds, however, combined these designs with a family record, and the four trees on either side of a cornucopia, the central motif, were taken from traditional sampler design. Examples like this had to be worked on a much coarser canvas than the designs embroidered in thinner threads. The Elizabeth Leeds sampler is on a linen canvas with twenty-six threads to the inch, much coarser than that of many early nineteenth-century samplers though still finer than modern needlepoint canvas. The com-bination of threads in this sampler, moreover, produces an interesting

effect. The Berlin designs and the four trees are worked in wool thread, but the family record blocks are done in silk, allowing for much finer lettering. A great many of the Berlin samplers were worked in wools, and special, imported German wools were available for these patterns. This woolwork is usually less fine than silk embroidery, but it often retains a great deal of its original color and, therefore, still looks striking today.

Lydia Platt's work (fig. 9), dated 1850, also demonstrates the combination of earlier traditional design with the less individual work of the mid-century. The motif of Solomon's Temple had been used on samplers as much as thirty years earlier, where it served as the central design, surrounded by floral arrangements, birds, cherubs, and other details, as already mentioned. Lydia Platt, however, was content to add only a row of very simple trees and two rather heavy flowers.

Beginning in the 1860s and through the period of the Centennial Exposition in 1876, the American sampler underwent dramatic changes. By the mid-1860s a nostalgic fascination with the American past encouraged the reproduction of earlier designs and forms in many of the decorative arts, and the sampler was no exception. In this period many samplers were created which follow the long, narrow shape of the seventeenth century. Unfortunately, these are often plain alphabet samplers done in wool threads on Penelope or double-thread canvas with meshes as wide as twenty-two threads to the inch. Often nothing more than a collection of alphabets, they do not attempt the delicate stitchery and balance of their earlier counterparts. For the most part, the stitches are limited to tent and cross stitch, with an occasional attempt at darning stitches.

About the time of the Centennial, punched-paper patterns for samplers became available. These had the design already marked out on heavy paper, with holes punched for the embroidery wool. They were available in a variety of patriotic and sentimental motifs and phrases—eagles, banners, the Liberty Bell, "What is Home without a Mother," "Rock of Ages," and many others, including even peacock and floral arrangements, presumably for the Pennsylvania-German market.

XXXX

The history of the American sampler is one of adaptation and innovation. The earliest examples were almost exact copies of their English counterparts, but as time went on this formalized, exact record of stitches was replaced by samplers that attempted pictorial and design elements in their own right. By the mid-eighteenth century both alphabet samplers, which were a conventional holdover from the earlier samplers, and more elaborate pictorial examples were being made.

American needleworkers have always been skillful at transferring designs and techniques from one medium to another, so all through the history of the sampler the same designs and techniques that were used in needlepoint, crewelwork, and silk-embroidered pictures were also to be found in samplers. Even in the Berlin-work period, many of the Berlin motifs and patterns were incorporated into traditional sampler designs.

Because the sampler was a domestic art, one practiced by women and girls with no expectation of monetary return, it was a form in which the artist was free to exercise individual expression. On the other hand, because samplers were so universally worked, they are particularly reflective of changing economic and social conditions, of cultural patterns and life styles. Because of their non-commercial nature as the product of women and girls at school or at leisure, samplers employed motifs and patterns taught by one generation to the next over and over again for periods of fifty or even 100 years. Except for variations in types of fabrics, the materials used and the methods of working remained substantially the same for centuries. This juxtaposition of convention with individual innovation encouraged the growth and practice of a continuing folk tradition, one to which we hope this study will contribute.

✖

DESIGN AND EXECUTION

✖

Our knowledge of how samplers were made, how the designs were planned, where the materials were obtained, and how the finished samplers were treated is very slender. Since the creation of samplers was a minor domestic occupation, rather than a commercial art, we have very little contemporary material about their planning and execution. The documents that exist for study in other areas of the decorative arts, such as cabinet-makers' price books, shop records, inventories, and account books do not exist for samplers. Contemporary advertisements for materials are usually too general to be of much help in determining exactly what materials were used and where they came from. The records and advertisements of schools seem to mention simply that "embroidery" or "needlework" is taught. Most of our information about the manner in which samplers were planned and executed has to be deduced from the samplers themselves, and therefore many of the tentative conclusions we reach can only be speculative.

Sixteenth- and seventeenth-century samplers were probably made by adult women, but as the sampler became less a working record and more a proof of basic skill, it was worked by younger girls. Although there are records of samplers worked by girls as young as five, the average age of eighteenth- and nineteenth-century sampler makers was about thirteen. In many instances the elaborateness of the work on a sampler, in relation to the age of the girl who made it, seems unbelievable to modern eyes, perhaps reflecting the great discipline expected by colonial culture of its young. Perhaps, however, the ages given on samplers are deceptive. In at least some cases a girl signed and dated her work as one of the first steps of her embroidery. The borders and signature block, usually in fairly simple stitches, were often completed first, the elaborate scenes being left for last. Several unfinished samplers that have been preserved substantiate this. If a girl worked on a sampler for a period of three or four years, as many may have done, she may have begun at twelve, and finished at fifteen.

We have no real way of knowing whether samplers were made by most young girls in the eighteenth and nineteenth centuries or whether this kind of work was done largely by upper- and middle-class girls. Some records and surviving samplers indicate that samplers were made in at least some charity schools and orphanages, but, since such institutions were not widespread before 1800, this does not tell us much about earlier samplers. Judging from the numbers in which they have survived, we can speculate that the making of a simple alphabet sampler was probably part of the domestic education of a great many girls in the late eighteenth and early nineteenth centuries. As the formal education of young women began to spread in the nineteenth century, more and more girls probably also learned the rudiments of fancy stitchery. For example, the large numbers of early nineteenth-century samplers surviving from the Delaware Valley is considered by some to be a result of Quaker support of the education of women at that time.

The more elaborate samplers were probably done largely by middle- and upper-class girls. These were a time-consuming pursuit, and a girl from a laboring family probably could not be spared from household duties for this kind of non-productive activity. Nor would the older women of such a household have had the spare time to supervise a project of this magnitude. Even if a girl from the poorer families was sent to school, her education almost certainly ended with primary school, and she did not have the opportunity to work a fancy sampler there. Once she was at home, she was needed in the dairy or at the loom.

In America, samplers and other embroidery were done almost exclusively by females. Recorded instances of samplers done by boys are very few. *American Samplers* lists only three, and one embroidered in wool on perforated cardboard by Nathaniel Palmer Stanton in 1861 is pictured in Georgiana Brown Harbeson's *American Needlework*.

The materials for most samplers were probably purchased. Most colonial households made and dyed their own wool yarn and linen cloth, but by far the most popular thread for sampler making was silk, which was largely imported, being cultivated only occasionally and experimentally in America. Indeed, it is very rare to find a sampler made before 1820 embroidered with anything but silk thread. The bright worsteds used in samplers made during the 1830s and '40s were also almost certainly imported.

Whether the linens on which the samplers were stitched were woven at home or purchased is an unresolved point. We can, of course, observe the cloth that was used, but we know little about its production. The width of the cloth, as well as the nature of the threads, may indicate that samplers were made on material especially manufactured for the purpose. We know that most early American households spun and wove great quantities of linen cloth, but not whether the cloth used for samplers was among that produced. Seventeenth-century samplers were stitched on very fine linen cloth, with as many as sixty-four threads to the inch. By 1800 the cloth was much coarser, generally from twenty-eight to thirty-six threads to the inch. Homespun linen sheets from this period have approximately the same thread count, but the cloth is much more closely woven than the sampler fabric—that is, the threads used are softer and thicker, so the sheets have a much tighter texture. We cannot gauge, however, how much of this soft texture is due to repeated washing, a process to which the sampler fabric has not been subjected. Sampler material of this period, however, does have a canvas-like texture not found in the sheets. It must be assumed either that special thread was spun at home to make cloth for samplers or that such cloth was purchased. By the nineteenth century, most samplers in the Delaware Valley were embroidered on the full width of the cloth—that is, they have two selvage edges, either the top and bottom or the two sides, usually the latter. With presently available evidence, however, we cannot determine whether looms were adjusted at home to make this cloth or whether the cloth was available from retail merchants. In New England, by contrast, samplers were often hemstitched on all four sides, but whether the hemstitching was done for its own sake, as part of the exercise of making the sampler, or out of necessity because the cloth was cut from a wider piece, we do not know.

The stitches used in antique samplers were many and varied. Cross stitch, satin stitch, and stem stitch are found on samplers from every age and every place. The combination of these three stitches, including all the many variations of cross stitch, can produce a surprising variety. Other stitches were used more selectively. Eighteenth-century examples sometimes incorporate various Florentine (bargello or flame stitch) motifs, which were popular for embroidery at the time. Alphabets, from the beginning of the mid-eighteenth century and continuing all through the nineteenth, are often done in eyelet stitch and star stitch, possibly to provide variety for the marking of linen. The rococo stitch was regularly used for strawberry borders in the Delaware Valley and the South in the late eighteenth and early nineteenth centuries. A close look at the strawberry border on Mary Ann Lee's sampler (fig. 10) will show that each strawberry is made up of a series of these tiny diamond-shaped stitches. Rococo stitch is ideally suited to the representation of the strawberry, with the open area of the stitch producing the same effect as the seeds of the fruit. Rococo stitch was also used in the Delaware Valley for small diamond-shaped motifs, another technique that can be observed in Mary Ann Lee's sampler. The stitch was also used in New England, in samplers done at Miss Polly Balch's school, where its tapestry-like effect was put to good use, as in the border flowers in Lydia Gladding's sampler (plate II). Strawberry borders in New England samplers, however, were usually done in cross stitch. Pictorial samplers made after 1820 were rarely done in anything other than cross, tent, or satin stitch. The most common sampler stitch, of all periods, is cross stitch.

The colors used in American samplers were generally strong and clear. We have already discussed the colors in the Mary Hollingsworth sampler (fig. 1) and the way in which one part of the original bright red color has been preserved. We can also see the use of clear red, green and blue, in addition to tans and browns, in Elizabeth Hudson's sampler of 1737 (plate I). The colors used most often were blues, greens, and roses. Yellow was used, sometimes in great blocks, but more often as an accent color. Clear reds were used all along, from the mid-seventeenth century. A great many tones of brown, rust, and tan were employed. Black, too, appears but less frequently than browns. There was very little use of purple and violets before the introduction of Berlin wools. Because the clear reds and roses in many early samplers have faded to rosy browns— the blues and greens keeping much more of their original colors—many early samplers give the impression of having been made in very quiet hues. An examination of the samplers pictured in the color plates, all in excellent states of preservation, as well as examination of the backs of samplers, shows that this is not so. The colors that were used had a certain subtlety because they were dyed with vegetable dyes, but they were by no means always subdued. Once samplers began to be worked in wools, as the Berlin-work craze spread, colors became more brilliant and harder. These samplers worked in wools, when placed against only slightly earlier silk-embroidered examples, give the effect today of being very bright because they have retained more of their original color.

Once sampler making ceased to be a method of recording stitch patterns and became an educational exercise, layouts and motifs were most likely planned by a relative or a teacher, rather than by the young girl who was stitching the sampler. Study of the backs of finished samplers and of unfinished examples suggests that cross stitch and other counted-thread elements must have been copied from charts because there is no indication of these designs having been drawn on the cloth. Satin stitch and other free-embrodiery elements, on the other hand, appear to have been drawn with fine marking ink. Two unfinished samplers in the Essex Institute show evidence of animals drawn on the cloth and intended to be completed in satin stitch (one squirrel is partly done). These elements were either drawn free-hand or were transferred from patterns by a method called pouncing. *The Dictionary of Needlework*, the great treasury of needlework terms and processes published in 1882, tells us how pouncing was done:

> Rub the Pounce [a finely powdered dark gum] over a piece of paper on which the pattern has been drawn, secure it firmly on the cloth, silk, or velvet to be embroidered, and prick the pattern through to the material beneath it, so as to deposit the Pounce upon it. Paint the outline with drawing liquid, which may be had in any colour.

There is no reason to suppose that this method of transferring changed much; the pouncing process was probably substantially the same 100 years earlier.

Whether antique samplers were embroidered in frames or with the fabric held in the hand is another unresolved question. Late eighteenth- and nineteenth-century embroidery frames exist today, but they are very rare. Their rarity, compared with similar household impedimenta like quilting frames, suggests that many women preferred to work with the fabric held in the hand, and that therefore few purchased frames. Perhaps, if frames were used, they were the property of the schools, where so many samplers of the period were worked, and were passed from pupil to pupil. The experience of the people who embroidered the new samplers for this book suggests that the quickest and most comfortable way to do counted-thread embroidery is with the fabric held in the hand, although most modern embroidery books insist that a frame must be used. Where antique frames have been found, they are often the adjustable stretcher type, either free-standing or held on the lap or a table. This type of frame allows the whole sampler to be stitched to tapes attached to the frame. Embroidery hoops may have been used for small sections of satin stitch and other stitches which require even tension on the fabric.

A good number of nineteenth-century samplers were framed, if not soon after they were made then at some time many years ago. It is rare today to find an elaborate sampler from the period 1770 to 1840 that has never been framed or exposed to light. Alphabet samplers, however, may or may not have been framed originally. The large number found today that were framed in the 1920s and '30s suggests that many of these were laid away and not considered suitable wall decorations until the interest in collecting "Americana" made them desirable curios. Frame styles, however, suggest that many of the more elaborate samplers from the early 1800s were not framed until the 1850s. On the other hand, some samplers were evidently framed when they were done: Betty Ring's article "Collecting American Samplers Today," which appeared in the June, 1972, issue of *Antiques*, illustrates a map sampler by Polly Platt of Athens, New York, dated 1809, bearing a frame labeled by Isaac L. Platt of New York City, probably a relative. Since Isaac was in business at the address on the label from 1815 to 1819, the sampler must have been considered important enough to send to the city to be framed a few years after it was made. The labels of several Federal looking-glass retailers and manufacturers indicate that they were ready to frame embroidery to order.

When a sampler was framed, it was usually simply stretched and tacked directly to the wooden backboard, although occasionally strips of cloth or tape were first stitched to the edges of the sampler. Although needlework pictures were sometimes attached to the backboard by drilling a series of tiny holes in the wooden board and then lacing the picture to it, samplers were rarely framed this way, perhaps because the linen on which they were worked was stronger and did not need the more careful handling of the needlework picture done on silk. Samplers from the 1860s and '70s were often framed, many in contemporary Victorian "rustic" frames with crossed corners, indicating that these were conceived initially as show pieces and nostalgic reminders.

As the study of samplers becomes less genealogically oriented and concentrates to a greater extent on design and techniques, more concrete evidence will undoubtedly become available about how they were planned and made. In the meantime, our very ignorance is tantalizing. Perhaps the next sampler donated to the local historical society or up at auction will contain a valuable clue to its method of execution. It is this possibility of discovery that adds excitement to the pleasures of viewing—and collecting—antique samplers.

✖

FORMING AND CARING
FOR A COLLECTION

✖

A collection of antique samplers can have as much or as little scope as the collector wants, and can cost a lot or a little. Samplers can provide a collection of exciting, original folk art at a fraction of the cost of a collection of paintings. Although fine eighteenth-century examples sold at nationally-advertised auctions often bring as much as several thousand dollars, good nineteenth-century pictorial examples can be bought in antiques shops and at auction at prices within the means of even a limited purse, and simple alphabet samplers can sometimes be bought for only twenty-five to thirty-five dollars.

Most people probably begin by buying a few inexpensive alphabet samplers, but you should not be afraid to branch out into the more interesting (and expensive) examples. A collection that consists only of ordinary pieces soon becomes uninteresting, except in terms of numbers. If you think that you can afford only inexpensive samplers, save the money whenever you are tempted and then buy one good example instead of six ordinary ones. In the end, a collection of six good samplers is more satisfying than twenty-five mediocre pieces.

Limiting your collection to one type of sampler or to samplers from one area can help you stay within a budget. If you try to collect only samplers that were made in a particular state or area, or only schoolhouse samplers, or only family-record samplers, you will discover that the challenge of finding examples and the unity of the collection will be adequate compensation for its small size. Do not be afraid to sell a sampler that your taste has outgrown. Perhaps the dealer from whom you are buying other samplers will buy it from you or will agree to sell it for you on consignment.

The two main sources for samplers are antiques shops and auctions. Begin by visiting the antiques shops and shows in your area. A little looking and questioning will give you some idea of the price range for various types of samplers. Look also at the classified sections in national antiques publications. If you live on the east coast, you can expect to find samplers in local household and estate auctions, although you will have to be prepared to go to many auctions in search of them. Read the auction ads in local papers and talk to people you meet at auctions to find out where other sales are advertised. Many auctioneers maintain a mailing list and will send you a handbill when they have a large or varied sale. Auction-going is a hobby in its own right, and if you aren't bitten by auction-fever you probably won't enjoy it, but small country and village sales are probably the only place where good, colorful nineteenth-century samplers can still be bought for under $100. The less money you have to spend, the more time you will have to spend hunting bargains.

If you live in an area where the country auction has vanished, you will have to buy from dealers or at consignment auctions. At a nationally-advertised auction of an important American folk art collection held in New York City in the winter of 1974, two excellent, colorful nineteenth-century samplers were sold for $300 and $400.

The further you live from the original centers of production, the more time, effort, and money you will have to invest in a collection of samplers. On the other hand, dealers do advertise modest pieces in national publications, and antiques shops and shows are everywhere, so you can, with patience, build a collection no matter where you live. Write to dealers who advertise samplers; many furnish snapshots for a modest fee, and most reliable dealers are willing to ship pieces with a return privilege. If you buy this way, be fair to the dealer. If she does not know you, the dealer has the right to expect payment before shipping. If you ask to see a piece on approval, and decide not to buy it, return it immediately, carefully packed and insured, so that the dealer can offer it to others. Once you have established a relationship of confidence with a dealer, you can expect to be notified when a piece comes in that fits your interests. Collecting is not just a matter of writing a check, but of study and appreciation of the things you collect. Examine your samplers closely—study the designs, the stitches, the fabric. Local historical societies can often help you find records of the girl who made the sampler if you have some idea of the area from which the sampler came.

As with any collection, keep records. Make notations in a card file or book of where you buy, how much you paid, and any other information you have. Either index your samplers in some way, or make a duplicate card with the information you have and attach it to the back of the frame. If you bought the sampler at auction, keep the auction catalogue or the newspaper ad with the sampler. This is not just a sentimental reminder but may be a great help to a future researcher who wants to track down the sampler's origin.

Look, read, and ask questions!

As soon as they are collected, most samplers need immediate attention. The two greatest enemies of antique needlework are acid and light. In order to preserve samplers in a manner that will allow for maximum visibility and at the same time afford maximum protection, there are some simple rules to follow.

If you purchase a sampler in its original frame, the frame should be removed so that the sampler may be taken off the wooden backboard to prevent the acids in the wood from eventually rotting the cloth. The backboard should be preserved, but something must be done to separate it from the sampler. The most satisfactory method is this: take a piece of pure linen or unbleached muslin, about four inches bigger all around the sampler. Wash the fabric, rinsing carefully, and iron it flat. Now carefully smooth the sampler flat on the cloth and pin in place. Attach the sampler to the cloth with long running stitches. Then cut a piece of acid-free, 100-percent rag matting board (available at most frame shops) to the size of the backboard, and stretch the sampler over it. The muslin or linen can be glued to the back of the mat board with white glue if necessary. In this way the sampler is supported, but it is not in contact with the wooden backboard. Since the sampler itself has been attached only to the muslin or linen, it can be removed at any time with no damage.

If the sampler is unframed or in an unsuitable frame, then the problem of finding a frame arises. Many people feel that since the original frame has been lost, the most acceptable substitute is a simple modern frame. Others believe that an antique frame suitable to the period of the sampler should be found. This is a question of personal taste. If you decide to look for an antique frame, you should study framed samplers in museums, antiques shops, and books in order to learn about the types of frames that might be appropriate.

Once you have found a suitable frame, the sampler can be mounted in the same way that a sampler is remounted in the original frame. If the frame is too large, it is wise to mount the sampler on acid-free, 100-percent rag board before taking the frame to be cut down. In this way, you can be sure that the dimensions will be right. If the backboards are missing, and the sampler needs more support, another piece of rag board can be used behind the first. It is probably a good idea, in any case, to seal the back of the frame with tape or brown paper, but in no case should the sampler be allowed to come in contact with any cardboard, paper, or matboard that is not 100-percent rag and acid-free.

If you buy a sampler that has been attached to the original backboard by the method of lacing the sampler to tiny holes drilled in the board, do not take it off the board in a hurry. Because this was an extremely unusual method of mounting a sampler, you should take the sampler to the textile department of the nearest large museum to seek advice. In any case, if the sampler must be removed, careful, detailed photographs should be taken, preferably by a professional photographer, so that a record of this rare mounting is preserved.

It is of the utmost importance to keep samplers out of direct sunlight. Even though the old vegetable dyes are stronger and faster than modern dyes, you can get a good idea of what will happen to a sampler in direct sunlight by looking at the fading that occurs in modern drapery fabric after as little as six months' exposure to direct sunlight. Hang your samplers on the wall, by all means, but make sure they are placed where direct sunlight will never strike them, even for a few minutes a day. If, for any reason, you will not be able to control where the sampler will be hung, take drastic precautions by having the glass in the frame replaced with a special ultra-violet screening plexiglass.

If a sampler is dirty, some thought should be given to cleaning it. There is always a risk involved in washing antique textiles, so weigh carefully before you begin. Fabrics can deteriorate, and colors run when wet. To be safe, it is better to leave the sampler dirty than to take the chance of damaging it. If you decide to wash a sampler, use plain, room-temperature water—no detergent, no Woolite, no Ivory Flakes. Do not crumble the sampler in the water, but use a pan large enough to let it lie flat in the water, or use the bathtub if necessary. Let the sampler soak for about fifteen minutes, then lift it out gently and roll in a turkish towel to absorb most of the moisture. Stretch and smooth the sampler on a flat surface covered with a dry towel and leave it to dry. If you must iron a sampler, place it face down on a turkish towel, cover with a very slightly damp cloth, and use a dry iron at low temperature.

If the sampler has holes in it, do not try to patch or mend it. Find an old piece of homespun linen that is as close in color and texture to the sampler as possible. Many antiques shops have remnants of homespun sheets or towels that they will sell cheaply. Simply sew the sampler onto the piece of homespun and let the homespun show through. If the holes are very large, you can take a few tiny running stitches to attach the backing linen.

There is nothing that can be done about faded color. Sometimes people attempt to touch up the colors in a sampler with felt markers or other coloring devices, but this not only destroys the character of the sampler; it is dangerous as well to the threads. Do not buy a sampler that has been touched up, and never try to touch up one you own.

Samplers that have to be stored temporarily should either be laid flat or rolled, never folded. The best method is to prepare the sampler as for mounting: by sewing it to washed, unbleached muslin or linen and laying it flat in a drawer between two sheets of tissue paper or cloth. If you roll a sampler around a cardboard tube, roll the tube in a piece of appropriate fabric first.

The safest and best advice about the conservation of old textiles is to do nothing in a hurry, do nothing that cannot be undone. If you are uncertain about what to do, as in the case of an unusual mounting method, take the sampler to the textile department of the nearest major museum and get professional advice before you do anything.

2

CREATING HISTORIC
SAMPLERS TODAY

All of the historic American samplers illustrated in the previous section of this book and those that can be seen in museums, private collections, and other books are, no matter what else may be said about them, the products of a very personal form of artistic expression. For a great many years following the mid-nineteenth century, sampler-making was largely laid aside by American women. Perhaps the home sewing machine, the availability of yards of factory-made embroidery trims, the greater insistence on equal education for boys and girls in the broader areas of universal knowledge, and the subsequent increasing liberation of women from the hearth, housework, and even home itself led to the decline of this, and other forms of handcraft.

In recent years, however, people seem to be dissatisfied with being surrounded by only the impersonal products of the machine age. More and more they want to see products of their own hands—not just for the products themselves, but for the pride of personal accomplishment that goes with something that is: that would not be but for themselves.

In the twentieth century we do not work samplers to have a permanent record of stitches and designs to use elsewhere (there are books available for that), nor do we have to do it ourselves if we want something decorative to hang on our walls. We do samplers for the pure joy in the rhythm of stitching, for the feel of the materials we are working with, for seeing the design take shape with each movement of the needle, for something pleasant to do in our leisure hours, and for the pride of accomplishment when the work is hung on the wall and admired by others.

Modern women usually start embroidering with a store-bought kit, a form of embroidery partly a personal exercise, but personal only in the technical aspects of the stitching itself since hundreds of other women will be stitching the exact same sampler in the exact same colors, size, and pattern. Certainly this is an easy way to start embroidering, but sooner or later you will want to carry a project through from beginning to end: from designing it, choosing materials for it, and stitching it, to framing and hanging it.

The following sections of this book were written to help you in that purpose. By using the general directions and the charted motifs and samplers, you should be able to create a very personal sampler in the historic tradition. You have four alternatives when you set about designing your sampler. You can find and copy an old sampler exactly, or you can alter that sampler to suit your size, design, and color requirements. You can create a sampler using motifs drawn from many sources, or you can design your own motifs.

Most historic samplers were done in counted-thread embroidery. In this work the background fabric is used much as the grid in graph paper is used in making graphs and charts, to count the stitches precisely, place them in the proper order, and make sure they are uniform in size. To modern needleworkers, probably the best known form of counted-thread embroidery is needlepoint, embroidery in wool which completely covers the surface of a canvas of evenly spaced threads. Needlepoint is usually worked in some form of a stitch that looks like half of a cross stitch, the stitch generally used for sampler making. Any chart designed for cross stitch can be used for needlepoint as well, and charts designed for needlepoint can be used for cross stitch. The time in doing both will be about the same since cross-stitch embroidery does not fill in backgrounds, but the stitch used for the motifs takes twice the time to do as the usual needlepoint stitch. The cost of materials will differ considerably, though, since more threads must be used to fill in the needlepoint background.

In many samplers some form of free embroidery is used along with counted-thread embroidery. In free embroidery the fabric forms a background only, with the size and direction of the stitches being dictated by the motif being stitched. Any fabric, countable thread or not, can be used for free embroidery. Instructions for this type of work are also included in the sections following.

✖

DESIGNING YOUR OWN SAMPLER

✖

Aside from the fact that most historic samplers are basically symmetrical in design and have some lettering on them, even if just a signature, not many more generalizations can be made about how they were designed and the design elements used. Some are made up of purely abstract shapes and stylized forms, others strive for reality. Some are delicate in design, others are bold. Just because a sampler is an antique does not mean that it is well designed. This book cannot give any formula for insuring a well-designed sampler. This must be your own endeavor, evolving from the study of historic samplers. What can be conveyed are some of the technical aspects of designing.

When planning your sampler, some of the things you should think about are:

1. How large your central design element (if there is one) will be

in relation to the design elements surrounding it, and to the size of the fabric itself. In simpler terms, what is to be the focal point of your sampler, and how will you make it the most important part? In some samplers it is a building, in others the signature or other lettering, or a scene with figures, or in some the framing border. Often samplers show a great disparity in normal scale between design elements. Sometimes a bird will be found sitting on a flower half its size, or a human figure will be as large as the three-story house next to it. This disparity in scale is eye-catching and lends a charming quality which somehow does not seem out of place.

2. Whether you will place your design elements close together or far apart, or where the heavier and more important elements will be. When the heavier elements are placed toward the center, or when the design elements are spaced farther apart, the sampler will have a more delicate look than when the heavier elements are placed toward the bottom and the other elements are placed closer together.

3. How your colors will be distributed on the fabric. Bright or dark colors become eye-catchers, and can keep the viewer's eyes in one place or send them moving around the sampler, depending on where they are placed.

4. Whether your design elements have a movement around the composition (see the lower section of the Adam and Eve family-record sampler in plate VIII) or are static (see the Pennsylvania-German sampler in plate VII).

5. Whether your design elements will be the same on both sides of the center line (symmetrically placed) or be different but related motifs, balanced by size and colors (asymmetrically placed).

Almost any kind of design will work for a sampler, whether modern or traditional, so long as one simple rule is followed. That rule is to simplify, simplify! Indicate, but do not describe important details. Cross stitch, the most commonly used sampler stitch, is purely geometric and looks best when used in terms of color and shape. Leave detail and texture for other stitches.

The equipment you will need for designing and graphing your own sampler includes large sheets (17″ x 22″) of graph paper in a grid of 10 squares per inch or more; tracing paper; colored pencils, markers, or drawing ink in a fountain pen (the kind of ink labeled "permanent" at stationery counters is not really permanent—only drawing ink is truly permanent in the sense that it does not smear when wet); and hot-iron transfer pencil or dressmaker's carbon paper. Graph paper, tracing paper, colored pencils or markers, and drawing ink can be purchased at art or drafting supply stores. Hot-iron transfer pencils can be bought at needlework stores, and dressmaker's carbon paper at most notion counters.

cornering borders

Very few historic samplers have framing borders that are cornered the same way on each of the four sides. If the young ladies who worked those samplers had wanted to corner them, they probably could have since some of the interior motifs are about as complicated to plan symmetrically as the borders. It possibly did not occur to them, or was not considered important. Whether or not the borders are symmetrically cornered on your sampler is purely a matter of taste. We prefer them perfectly cornered, and the three of our adapted samplers that have borders are done that way.

If your sampler is to have a symmetrically-cornered border, the rest of your sampler will have to be designed after the border is graphed out so that it will fit within the border frame with no obviously empty or crowded spaces. The border you choose will have a certain number of stitches in each repeat of the undulating line, which is the basic design element in most sampler borders. Some will have as few as ten stitches to a repeat, others as many as seventy-seven stitches. Naturally, it will be far easier to fit a border with a smaller repeat into the desired size of the sampler and still corner it symmetrically.

On the graph paper draw a rectangle or square that is the same number of stitches tall and wide that the finished sampler is to be. In pencil, graph one corner and then the undulating line of the two sides that meet at that corner. As each line gets to its next limit, see if the corner will fit the preliminary outline of the sampler. If it comes out exactly, great! If it is only a few stitches off, don't lose heart because you can easily add or subtract a few empty rows in the interior. If it is way off, see if you can add or subtract one stitch from each repeat of the undulating line to make it fit, or change the dimensions of the sampler to fit the border, or choose another border.

If you have found a border in another source that is not cornered, or is cornered badly, you can do a good cornering job in no time at all. You will need a mirror without a border or frame, one that can reflect down to the very edge. Stand the mirror on edge on the straight border at a 45° angle to it. Move it up and down the border until you have found a place where it makes a perfect right angle in the border without cutting any flower in half or leaving too much space between flowers. Use the mirror as a straight edge and draw a line at that 45° angle. Now all you have to do is graph the border, turning the corner where the line has indicated.

graphing lettering

No matter how you decide to stitch your sampler—whether in satin stitch, cross stitch, or the numerous other stitches which can be scattered throughout the piece—no matter what design elements you will include, you will want to sign, date, and place your work in cross stitch. While the sampler is in the designing stage you may not see the need to worry about signing your name, feeling that if there is any room when the stitching is completed you might just squeeze in your initials somewhere. Reject that thought immediately! The signature in most historic samplers is an integral part of the overall design and should be so in your sampler. (See especially the Pennsylvania-German sampler in figure 11 and our adaptation in plate VII.)

There is a great deal of satisfaction in signing your work. A signature adds a special uniqueness and charm to a sampler and makes it more valuable both historically and intrinsically. Knowing where and when you made your sampler will make it even more interesting and valuable in future years. From a historical standpoint, the more informative lettering there is on a sampler, the more valuable it becomes to the owner, especially if the original needleworker was an ancestor. If you are making a sampler to give as a gift, you could even stitch the name of the recipient along with your own.

If possible you should graph out your complete name before designing the rest of the sampler. Lettering takes up an amazing amount of space in stitchery, and since lettering cannot be easily changed while other smaller motifs can, it is wise to lay in your complete signature or other lettering first, or at least have a general idea where it will be placed and what will be placed around it.

First, simply print all your lettering as you want it to appear—for instance, name on one line, place on a second line, date on a third. Choose an alphabet either from the examples charted in this book or from one you have charted yourself from a printed source like an artist's lettering book. Count the number of cross stitches in the width that each individual letter will take, and mark that number underneath its corresponding printed letter. Add a number 1 for the blank space between each printed letter, and at least 2 blank spaces between each word. Do not forget commas and periods. Take the total of the numbers on each individual line.

Now refer back to your fabric and roughly block out the space in the width that will be needed for the longest line of lettering. To do this divide the number of cross stitches per inch that the thread count of your fabric permits into the number of spaces taken up on the graph paper by the line of lettering. For instance, lettering that takes up 87 spaces on graph paper will occupy a little over 7″ on fabric of 24 threads to the inch, 12 cross stitches to the inch. If this seems well within the limits of the space, measure the height of the entire block lettering. When figuring this dimension add the number of spaces below the line that letters such as g, p, q, and y will take, plus at least 1 empty row between each line of lettering. Roughly block this dimension on your fabric. If it also works, you can proceed to the next step.

If the block of lettering is too small, you could consider working the alphabet you have chosen in cross stitch over more than 2 threads (check to make sure your embroidery thread will cover the fabric well in this new stitch dimension); in another stitch which uses more threads, such as eyelet or crossed corners stitch; enlarging it by adding more empty spaces between each letter and word; adding more design motifs around it; or choosing another, larger alphabet. If you have chosen to work the lettering in a stitch which takes more than 2 threads, you will first have to determine how many of those stitches will fill 1″ of your fabric, and then determine again how much space each line of lettering will fill on your fabric. For instance, lettering that takes up 87 spaces on graph paper will occupy close to 11″ on fabric of 24 threads to the inch, 8 stitches to the inch when done in cross stitch over 3 threads.

If the lettering takes up too much room using the smallest alphabet, consider eliminating some other design motifs around it, or working the alphabet in cross stitch over a single thread. To find out how much fabric space working over a single thread will take, chart as usual on the graph paper, remembering that each space on the paper will now indicate 1 fabric thread instead of 2. For instance, lettering that takes up 87 spaces on graph paper will occupy a little over 3½″ on fabric of 24 threads to the inch when done in cross stitch over a single thread.

When you have settled on the alphabet and stitch to be used, divide the total number of spaces for each line in half and determine where that will be on the printed lettering. Mark a center line on the graph paper and copy the letters onto it, working from the center of each line toward either side. Any easily-read symbol, colored pencil, or marker can be used to indicate each stitch. When stitching the lettering onto the fabric, a guideline thread stitched down the center will help place the lines of letters symmetrically on either side of the center. When stitching letters, work as you did when graphing them—from the center toward either side—to insure proper placement.

graphing designs from various sources

There comes a time when every embroiderer wants to test her own creativity, when working designs prepared by others is no longer interesting or exciting. The only alternative to wishing is to do it yourself.

Drawing a design for needlepoint directly on canvas is fine, because if you make a mistake you can paint over it, repaint, and then cover design and background totally with stitches, removing all telltale signs of error. On a sampler it is a different story. Since only the design is stitched and the background is the fabric itself, a mistake in drawing can be fatal, not to mention costly. Probably no one has a steady enough hand to take that risk.

Your first step, then, is to get some large sheets (17″ x 22″) of graph paper. Now count the threads per inch on your fabric and divide by 2. That will be the number of worked cross stitches per inch, assuming that each cross stitch covers a square of 2 threads each way. The graph paper that is most available has a grid of 10 squares per inch. This grid matches up with embroidery fabric having 20 threads per inch, 10 cross stitches per inch. Except for this instance, you will rarely find graph paper to match exactly the number of cross stitches per inch that your fabric has, so some compensating will have to be done on the graph paper.

Let us say you have chosen a fabric that has 24 threads per inch, 12 cross stitches per inch. Your graph paper has 10 squares per inch, each square representing 1 cross stitch. Obviously the graphed design will be larger than the stitched design (two sheets of paper may have to be taped together to get one sheet large enough). This disparity of size is of no consequence if you first block out an area on the graph paper equal to the number of cross stitches available on the fabric. If the area on the fabric is 17″ wide by 18″ long, multiply each of these dimensions by 12 to find that there will be 204 cross stitches in the width and 216 cross stitches in the length. On the graph paper, block out an area 204 squares by 216 squares. This will work out to 20.4 inches by 21.6 inches. No matter that this is larger than the fabric area—the scale is correct. This method is to be used if you are designing your sampler from scratch to fit the dimensions of your fabric. If you are reproducing a historic sampler on graph paper or wish to design freely, the process is reversed, fitting the number of cross stitches on the fabric to match the number indicated on the chart after the chart is completed. Either way, once the design is charted on the graph paper, if each square is carefully reproduced on the fabric as 1 cross stitch, the sampler will be an exact stitched version of the graph.

Now to the actual charting. If you are fortunate and are able to get nose to nose with a historic sampler for any length of time, you can count stitches from the sampler to the graph paper—color by color, stitch by stitch, row by row, motif by motif—using colored pencils or the types of symbols for each color that are used in this book. Count the empty spaces, too, for an exact thread-by-thread reproduction.

Getting that close to historic samplers is not always easy. Museums which have large collections do not always have them on public view, and major private collections are almost totally inaccessible. A fine alternative is to buy or rent the slides that many museums have. Project the slide on a blank white wall and sit at a table with your graph paper directly in front of you beneath the projection. If the slide is very good, each stitch will seem to stand out in bold relief, and since the projection will probably be larger than the actual dimensions of the sampler itself, charting from the projection may even be easier than working from the actual sampler.

If you wish to design your own sampler from scratch, you may pick and choose from the section of charted motifs presented in this book, or you may design and chart your own motifs. Sources for motifs may be found everywhere, not just in needlework but in all forms of art and graphics, antique and modern.

In Chart XVII the figure of a woman carrying two baskets, dressed in a straw hat and long lavender dress with a red shawl, was not taken from any sampler, but was adapted from a tracing of a watercolor of the period. The large brick building in Chart XIII was not found on a sampler either, but was drawn from a modern photograph of a house built by Samuel McIntire of Salem, Massachusetts, in the late eighteenth century.

Historic samplers depicting horses are relatively rare, but if you want to show one, remembering that horses and other animals on historic samplers are reduced to their barest details and most recognizable silhouettes, it is easy to find a simple drawing and put it into graph form. Many such line drawings are available in children's coloring books and illustrated story books. The horse on Chart XII is taken from an illustration accompanying the nursery ryhme "I Had a Little Pony," which was found in a thirty-nine cent coloring book. The running stag at the bottom left of Chart XII was adapted from a drawing found on a package of Instant Quaker Oatmeal.

You can easily graph any conceivable picture by rendering a simplified line drawing of the original on your graph paper and then stepping the curved lines of each color area along the squares of the graph paper. All that remains is to indicate the different colors by different symbols or colored pencils. Match the number of stitches in the length and width of your fabric to the corresponding number of squares in the graph, and proceed to your stitching. Remember that to be effective as stitchery many details and subtle curves must be deleted from the original, although the larger the graphed design is (that is, the greater the number of stitches in each design), the more details and subtle curves may be added.

enlarging and reducing designs

In most cases the motif that you pick to graph from an outside source will be either too small or too large for the space available for it. When that happens, the size of the drawing will have to be enlarged or reduced to fit the space. You could take the drawing and have it photostated to your exact dimensions or have it done for free and in no time at all by doing it yourself.

To enlarge or reduce a design to a size suited to the space available on your graph paper corresponding to that same space on the sampler, first draw a square around the edges of the original drawing. Next divide this frame into squares of equal size. Now draw a square of the required new size and divide it into the same number of equal-sized squares. Areas within individual squares on the original drawing which have a lot of detail may be further subdivided into equal squares. The corresponding squares within the new size frame will also be further subdivided. Working freehand, it will be possible to draw the design in the new frame square by square, faithfully repeating the lines and proportions of the original design.

Enlarging and reducing designs by the above method is purely a mechanical skill which is learned much as you would learn a new stitch and does not take any special artistic talent. Knowing how to do it is as important a tool to the designing embroiderer as the needle and should not be feared by anyone.

If the change in size was done for cross-stitching, trace the design onto graph paper, block out the stitch squares, and proceed as usual.

adapting designs to satin stitch

If perhaps you find a design you like, but prefer to work in satin stitch, first determine the space available for it on the sampler itself. Enlarge or reduce the design to the required size by the method described in the preceding paragraphs. If the design you want to adapt for satin stitch is already graphed as for cross stitch, choose either of the two following methods for transferring the design to your fabrics. If it is a drawing or picture, follow the second method only. (In this case the need for curving stepped edges is eliminated.)

1. Outline each color area from the charted design onto your fabric in a light sewing thread, counting threads and stitches from the chart. Backstitch can be used for this procedure. Then proceed with the stitching in satin stitch, curving the stepped edges that are naturally caused by cross stitch. Using this method, your embroidery can be more free, and you will be able to make changes as you stitch if you feel the design warrants changing. When the stitching is completed, carefully clip and pull out the sewing thread that was used as a guide.

2. Trace the design lightly onto tracing paper with a regular semi-hard pencil, curving the stepped edges. Turn the drawing to the reverse side and trace over the penciled design with a special hot-iron transfer pencil (available in red and blue for around one dollar). Your drawing must be a mirror image of the original to transfer correctly. Be careful when using the transfer pencil to keep the point very sharp, the lines quite thin, and the paper free from any smudges because all lines will widen and smudges will be transferred to your fabric. Pin, then baste, the tracing face down on the fabric and press with a hot iron. Do not move the iron around while it is resting on the fabric. Rather, lift it up carefully and move it to the next area to be transferred. It would be a good idea to do a small sample first to see how hot your iron should be. When the ironing is completed, remove the paper and your design will be clearly marked on the fabric. Since the transfer design on your fabric is marked in only one color, you may work from the original drawing in choosing your colors or you may change and add colors as you stitch. Proceed with your stitching, making sure that your stitches cover the lines of the transferred design since these lines are usually permanent.

Dressmaker's carbon paper is not as successful as a transfer pencil in transferring designs and marking in detail on the relatively coarse and bumpy surface of embroidery linen. You would also be working blindly, not being able to see exactly what you are marking until all the marking is finished. If a mistake is made it is quite difficult to realign the drawing, because the opaque carbon paper obscures your view of the fabric. Regular typing carbon paper tends to smear and smudge while the design is being worked and handled and should never be used.

Some sampler kits may be bought where the background fabric has too many threads per inch to count threads for cross stitch. Each cross stitch is therefore indicated on the material by the use of a transfer pattern. No colors are shown on this stamped fabric but are indicated on a chart or picture that goes with the kit. It is possible to prepare fabric this way at home, marking graph paper with crosses done with a transfer pencil, then ironing the network of crosses onto a fine fabric. However, a sampler made in this way will always look mass-produced, without the refinement and definitive placement of each stitch that are the hallmarks of fine counted-thread embroidery. Besides, it hardly seems worth all the extra effort it would take to work out the chart, reverse it, then painstakingly mark it with crosses with the transfer pencil, which would constantly have to be sharpened. It would probably take as long to stitch as a sampler done by the counted-thread technique anyway since you would still constantly have to refer back to the chart for proper color placement. It may be an acceptable way to get a decorative piece of needlework up on your wall, but the product will never be the fine stitchery you would want to show off as your personally designed and executed sampler.

✖

MATERIALS

✖

fabric

Since the sampler that you ultimately work will involve a great deal of time, effort, and some expense, the materials you choose should be the very best.

Before setting out to buy your fabric and threads you should have graphed the design you will stitch and know the relative size you wish the sampler to be. (Do not forget to add 6″ to each dimension when figuring the size of the fabric.) This knowledge will almost dictate the thread count of the fabric you buy, which will in turn dictate the size or weight of the embroidery thread you buy. There are other considerations though. Will there be large masses of solid color, such as a building or a lawn, or will there be smaller scattered flower or bird motifs and a more delicate look to the design? Is the sampler to be large, yet contain relatively few design elements, or is it to be small and contain many design elements? If the look is one of great delicacy, perhaps silk or pearl cotton should be used on a fabric with a high thread count. If the look is bold, then perhaps wool or heavy matte-finished cotton thread worked on a fabric with a low thread count should be your choice. Let your design dictate the materials to use. In most cases the choice will be obvious.

The fabric that you choose should first of all be of an even weave; that is, it should have the same number of threads in the length as in the width. If they are not the same, each motif will be distorted. The weave should also be fairly close. This is especially important if you decide to work with a fabric of 24 or fewer threads to the inch, because if the threads are too far apart the sampler will not have a good finished surface since each cross stitch will pull greater holes in the fabric. The lower the thread count, the thicker the fabric threads should be as long as they are easily countable.

There should be no imperfections such as pulled or torn threads or knots. A certain nubbiness or slight variation in the width of individual thread in some linens is not considered an imperfection but a different surface texture which can be quite pleasing. Whatever fabric you choose, it should not hang limp in your hand, or be too stiff, but should have some body or crispness.

When having any fabric cut from the bolt, be sure that it is cut along a single thread on both cut ends. If it is not, you could lose as much as three inches in trimming it evenly.

Linen has been the universal choice of embroiderers for hundreds of years. It wears well, works well, and has lovely and varied surface qualities. Linen for counted-thread embroidery can be bought today in widths ranging from 13 inches to 71 inches, in thread counts of from 14 per inch to 36 per inch, at prices ranging from four dollars a yard to eighteen dollars a yard. Although linen fabric is now available in almost the entire spectrum of colors, the embroiderer wishing to do a sampler in the historic tradition would be well advised to pay attention to colors listed in needlework catalogs as natural, cream, beige, ivory, ecru, oatmeal, fawn, and white. Most fine linen embroidery fabric found in retail stores today has been imported from Switzerland, France and Scotland, or the Scandanavian countries, and can be bought by quarters of a yard as well as by the full yard. This might be important if the fabric you choose is one of the more expensive ones.

Cotton fabric has also long been used for counted-thread embroidery. The Museum of Primitive Art in New York City has in its collection a sampler from Peru worked in straight stitches on cotton, circa 200 B. C. The embroiderer should not be afraid that cotton will not hold up well!

There are two kinds of cotton fabric, mercerized and unmercerized. Mercerized fabric has been preshrunk and given a surface sheen by treating it with sodium hydroxide. The most popular cotton fabrics for embroidery are 22 thread-count Hardanger cloth (11 cross stiches per inch), where each vertical and horizontal thread is actually 2 threads lying side by side, and Ida or Aida cloth, a basketweave cloth of 11 or 14 threads per inch. Because each of those individual 11 or 14 threads is made up of 4 interlocked threads, you work cross stitch over only a single composite thread, so on this fabric there will be 11 or 14 cross stitches per inch.

If you are working your first piece of counted-thread embroidery, do not be overzealous and start working on a fabric with an extremely high thread count. Try to limit yourself to a fabric which is less demanding, such as Hardanger cloth or an 18 to 24 thread-count linen.

In the mid-nineteenth century some samplers were done on a fabric that approximates what is known today as Penelope or double-mesh canvas. In modern needlepoint the entire surface of this canvas is covered with tent stitches, but in most nineteenth-century samplers the backgrounds were left bare, and only the designs worked. Although this kind of a sampler will be easy to stitch, the effect will not be as pleasing as work done on linen fabric because the open spaces will look coarse and unfinished. You can, however, work your sampler on modern needlepoint canvas and fill in the entire background to produce an effect like that of Mary Wiggin's sampler (plate IV) or Lydia Gladding's (plate II).

When choosing materials for such a sampler, Penelope canvas of 10 mesh should be the largest you consider. You would work cross stitches or tent stitch over each double intersection of threads and therefore have 10 stitches to the inch, or work tiny stitches over a single intersection of threads for special effects or lettering (petit point) and have 20 stitches to the inch. Both kinds of stitching can be combined on the same sampler, but you would have to adjust the thickness of your embroidery thread to the different dimensions of the two kinds of stitching.

Penelope canvas can be worked in the same threads that are used to work linen or cotton fabric, but the most universally used thread, both in the nineteenth century and today, is Persian wool. Silk can be combined beautifully with wool for special effects and highlights, especially when working some areas in petit point. A great many stitches can be used on canvas, and some can be considered for filling in backgrounds. Consult some good needlepoint books for more stitches than are described in this book.

needles

In all counted-thread embroidery the needle should not actually pierce the fabric, but should slip through the holes between the fabric threads. Therefore blunt- or rounded-tipped tapestry needles with relatively large eyes are used for cross stitch. These seem to roll off the threads into the holes and help the working of the embroidery to move swiftly and easily. Sharp, pointed embroidery or crewel needles are intended for actually piercing fabric and are suitable for working in satin stitch on fabrics of very fine mesh or thread count.

Tapestry needles with large eyes and blunt tips are available in sizes 13 (large) to 26 (small). Crewel needles with sharp tips and long eyes are available in sizes 1 (large) through 10 (small). Chenille needles have the large eyes of tapestry needles and the sharp points of crewel needles. They are useful for doing satin stitch in wool. They are sized the same way as tapestry needles.

No matter what kind of needle you are using, no needle should be left in the sampler fabric when the work must be put down, especially not anywhere in the face of the sampler. No matter how good the needle, it will rust in time, even from the humidity in the air, and leave spots on the fabric. If you must put down your work in a hurry, and have no other place to put your needle, at least put it through the hem of the fabric. The best place for your needle, however, is in a special felt needle-book which you can sew into your thread roll (see page 65).

For a needlebook, cut two squares of felt, one a little larger than the other. Sew these together down the middle. Fold them as you would a book, with the smaller piece on the inside. Sew a snap in the center of the inside faces of the larger piece, and store your needles only in the smaller inside piece.

threads

The threads available to today's embroiderer come in almost endless sizes, weights, textures, and colors. Sometimes the vast range that is available makes choosing your particular threads a difficult task. Knowing the relative weight and texture of the threads with which your fabric and design can successfully be worked makes the choice a little easier.

It is a good idea, though not necessary, to make up a little sample book containing swatches of embroidery fabrics and small skeins of threads in basic colors. Just paging through your sample book can inspire design ideas. You might find yourself designing your sampler to be worked in particular threads and fabrics that you favor.

Most thread manufacturers put out color cards for each type of thread they sell. These contain small samples of each color available in the various types of thread, and can sometimes cover as many as 300 colors. These cards can be bought at fairly low prices and are handy to have for planning your color schemes at home, perhaps to be sure they complement the colors of the room in which the sampler will eventually be hung, while staying within the traditional color range. They can also be used when visiting collections of historic samplers to make accurate notes on colors in them. It is much more precise to note that the pink used in a particular motif was close to color number 295 on the Paragon Peri-Lusta color chart than to merely state that it was a medium rose-pink.

The most available thread, and one of the least costly, is stranded embroidery cotton, also called cotton floss, which can be bought at five and ten cent stores. It comes in an almost limitless range of colors and can be split to any size to fit your particular stitches and fabric. It has a slight sheen and when worked neatly can produce a lovely surface. When more than one of its 6 strands are used, the individual strands sometimes tend to move separately in the needle and tangle easily, so some extra care must be taken to keep the strands neat. It can be bought in over 300 colors in skeins containing about 9 yards.

There are 4-ply, matte-finished heavy cotton threads, one type of which is divisible, one which is not. Suitable for work on canvas as well as on fabric, they are put up in 11-yard skeins, come in over 100 colors each, and are moderately expensive.

A matte-finished, single-strand twisted cotton from Denmark, called Blomstergarn, or Flower Thread, is put up in 33-yard skeins in close to 100 lovely, soft colors. It may be multiplied in the needle for a heavier weight thread.

There is, of course, pearl cotton, which is a twisted thread with a beautiful high gloss. It comes in weights ranging from 1 (the thickest) to 8 (the finest). Sizes 5 and 8 are the most widely used for cross-stitch and satin-stitch embroidery. Pearl cotton hardly ever tangles and is incredibly easy to work with, its only problem being a tendency to fluff with excessive handling. Size 8 is put up in 95-yard balls, and size 5 in 53-yard balls. Both come in over 100 colors and are inexpensive. Pearl cotton was used for three of the four adapted samplers in this book.

Embroidery silk is not readily available today, but can be bought if you search hard enough. A stitched surface in silk is brilliant, with absolutely glowing colors. Most silk comes from France and Switzerland in small skeins of divisible threads (much like stranded-cotton floss) and is quite expensive. It is slippery in the needle and tends to tangle easily, so great care must be taken to keep the strands neat. There is also a matte-finish silk embroidery floss. An alternative to embroidery silk is silk buttonhole twist which can be bought at most fabric stores put up on 10-yard spools. The color range is not as extensive as in embroidery silk, but the thread is relatively inexpensive.

Synthetic threads are fairly easy to work with, but, oddly, are not yet widely available. If you can find them, there are Oiska, a heavy, glossy rayon thread from Denmark; Globo, a synthetic silk from Mexico; and Bella Donna, a synthetic silk from Germany.

A linen thread from Sweden, called Linda, is available in about 100 colors. It must be worked in very short lengths to keep its surface neat and shiny. It is put up in 12-yard skeins and is moderately expensive.

Most modern wool threads, color-fast and usually moth-proofed, come in hundreds of colors in large color families and are relatively inexpensive. Tapestry and embroidery wool, crewel wool, and Persian wool are available almost everywhere. Most are capable of being doubled and tripled, or stripped down to one or two threads for an exact fit to the stitch and fabric. A single thread could conceivably be used on fine fabric, but wool looks best in double or triple weights on fabrics with lower thread counts.

It is best to buy all the thread required for a piece of needlework at once. Most needlework stores will take returns on unused, unopened skeins (keep your receipt), so it is wise to get more than enough, rather than find you have too little when you have almost finished your sampler. When buying yarn or thread, be sure to get it all from the same dye lot, for colors vary slightly from dye lot to dye lot. Most salespeople in needlework stores are knowledgeable about thread requirements and will help you to figure out how much of each color you will need. These requirements will depend on the size of the sampler, the type of stitch predominating (some stitches require more thread than others), the thread count of your fabric, the number of strands you will use in your needle, how much of each color is used, and the number of yards in each skein or ball.

There are places to buy embroidery materials other than retail needle-work stores. Stores that sell large quantities of upholstery and drapery materials sometimes have lovely linen and cotton fabrics of even thread count suitable for working cross stitch. At antique auctions, flea markets, antiques shops, rummage and yard sales, whole cartons of old or antique linen and homespun fabrics are often sold at nominal prices. At a recent church rummage sale an ecru 100-percent linen tablecloth with 28 threads per inch was bought for twenty-five cents. It is at least fifty years old (admittedly not an antique, but with some age) and has a look and soft-ness that modern fabrics do not have. It has a torn corner, but at least three usable yards of fine embroidery fabric. This tablecloth has obviously been laundered many times and has held up very well, but any older fabric like this should be treated with the same care given antique samplers.

It is even possible to buy embroidery threads far afield. Ten large reels of pre-World War II fine Japanese embroidery silk in glorious, glow-ing colors were bought at a flea market for one dollar for the lot and contain enough precious thread to provide a lifetime of stitching.

storage of threads

Once you have started to do any kind of needlework, you will find that you are building a palette of threads of various kinds and colors and that their storage can become a problem. How to keep the threads sorted, neat, and tangle free, yet easily accessible is a question many embroiderers face. There are numerous solutions for permanent storage, but one of the best is to separate the threads into color families and knot the working lengths loosely with a lark's head knot—the kind of knot used in fasten-ing price tags—over an extra large wire hanger, the kind on which cleaners sometimes deliver bedspreads and draperies. These hangers— made of extra thick wire, with the lower horizontal section covered by a thick cardboard tube—can be hung in your clothes closet with a piece of cloth draped over them to keep the threads dust free.

To keep the palette you are working with at the moment neat and readily accessible, not in a tangled jumble at the bottom of your embroidery basket, there are also many solutions. A rectangular piece of cloth with two lengths of twill tape—one at the top, one at the bottom—sewn down at half-inch intervals in small loops through which the thread is pulled in color families, will keep the threads neat and even dust free, for it can be rolled up when not in use.

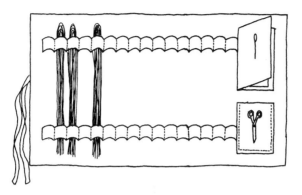

It would be a good idea to include somewhere in your thread roll a little needlebook like the one described on page 62 so that your needle may be left there and not in the sampler when not in use. If left in the sampler it may rust and stain the material.

The thread roll could also include a small pocket for storage of scissors, thimble, measuring tape, and anything else you might require.

The outside of such a thread roll could be decorated with a sampler of various embroidery stitches.

Another version of the thread roll, though not so durable, is made by stapling half-inch elastic to heavy paper such as oaktag.

The easiest method of storing threads for current work is to use the inside ring of a small unused embroidery hoop through which the working lengths of thread are loosely knotted, as over the heavy hanger for permanent storage. This is not recommended for fine and precious threads such as silks and metallics, but is fine for wool and cotton threads.

miscellaneous aids

Some materials which traditional instruction books say are obligatory in doing fine needlework are just a nuisance to many embroiderers. Many needleworkers never become accustomed to a thimble and embroidery hoop or frame and refuse to use them, but continue nevertheless to stitch fine pieces of needlework.

The four women who worked the four adapted samplers shown in plates VII-X all started work with an embroidery hoop because they felt they were supposed to. Within a few days the hoops had found their various ways to the bottoms of four workbaskets, to be brought out only when large areas of satin stitch were to be done. Only one of the women used a thimble.

The proper use of a hoop or frame requires that each stitch be done with two hands and in two separate movements. Working in two movements means that each stitch will take twice as long to complete, each cross stitch done in four movements rather than two movements. Consequently, the entire sampler will take twice as long to complete. Loosening the fabric in the frame or hoop so that the stitch can be worked with one hand in one movement obviates its use. Speed is not necessarily essential, but no embroiderer can be excited for long about a project which seems to go on forever. Many embroiderers are already designing their next piece of work in their heads while stitching the present one and are anxious to get on with it.

Some people cannot pick up a needle without a thimble: its use is so essential to their stitching; others literally cannot pick up a needle while using a thimble: their hands feel so clumsy and helpless with it on. If you do use a thimble be sure that it fits correctly, or it will be more of an annoyance than an aid.

All that can be said is that if using a thimble and hoop slows you down and makes stitching unpleasant, by all means put them aside. But if you feel comfortable using these materials, by all means do so.

If you prefer working in a hoop or frame, there are many to choose from. Round hoops come in wood, metal, and plastic, but the one preferred by most expert embroiderers is the wooden one with a screw on the outer ring so that the tension on the fabric can be varied. To prevent marring worked stitches that will fall within the two rings, the inner ring can be wound round with tape, or a piece of tissue can be laid over the fabric before putting it in the hoop, then torn away on the stitching surface after the screw has been tightened.

Embroidery frames are made of four pieces of wood, two having webbing attached to which the cut edges of the fabric are sewn, and the other two having holes drilled through which the selvage edges of the fabric are laced.

Besides the small hoop which is held in the hand, there are hoops which stand on the floor, sit on a table, screw to the edge of a table, and a new type which is held in place by means of a board upon which the embroiderer sits. If you work with a hoop, all these devices are necessary to free both hands for working, for in a hoop or frame you must push the needle through the fabric with one hand and bring it back up to the surface with the other.

Although hand-held hoops can be carried about, using a standing hoop or frame cuts down on the portability of your work. Some embroiderers, however, feel that any fine piece of needlework which is slated to become an heirloom should not be carried around from place to place where it could conceivably meet with accidental disaster. They believe it would be best to keep such a piece in a special place where it can be both worked on and stored, covered by a piece of muslin. Others just roll their unframed work and drop it in their work basket or bag to take with them wherever they go.

Be sure to have in your workbasket a good sharp pair of scissors to be used exclusively for embroidery. Embroidery scissors are usually about three inches long with sharp-pointed tips, and some fine folding models are available today.

A tape measure or long ruler is a necessity, and a six-inch ruler is handy to have.

A plain sewing thread and needle should be in your workbasket for putting in guideline stitching as it is needed.

For very fine stitching there is a large magnifying glass which hangs from the neck and is propped up on the chest to make stitching more visible. It is an invaluable aid to embroiderers who have problems with close work.

✖

STITCHES

✖

cross stitch

Cross stitch is the universal stitch of samplers, appearing even on ancient native samplers from Thailand. It is probably the first stitch any child learns and, like bicycle riding, once learned is never forgotten.

Cross stitch is actually two stitches, the second diagonal stitch crossing the first diagonal stitch at a right angle to it. Before learning the stitch, two rules must be impressed. First, each complete cross stitch throughout the entire sampler must be worked over the same number of threads of the fabric, usually 2, but acceptable over more. Second, the top stitch in each cross on the entire sampler must cross in the same direction, usually from lower left to top right, as in the slant in handwriting. Otherwise the work will have a messy appearance.

There are two methods of working cross stitch, the first being preferred by experienced needleworkers because of its more uniform appearance.

1. Work each cross stitch of 2 slanting stitches, the first from lower right to upper left, the second crossing it from lower left to upper right. Work each stitch completely before moving on to the next.

Letter A *in cross stitch*

2. Work half of each cross stitch in one line, then make a return trip, completing each stitch with the top layer of the cross.

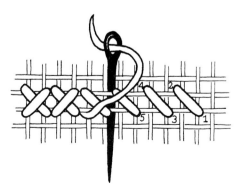

Since the second method produces a slightly different surface than that obtained by completing each stitch individually (especially when working with wool), it is advisable to use it only in isolated long rows, as in borders. In cross stitching, regularity and evenness of the surface is to be worked for at all costs.

crossed corners stitch

Crossed corners stitch is a fancy variation of cross stitch. Here a regular cross stitch is made over 2 fabric threads, although it could be made over 4 fabric threads in a heavier embroidery thread. Then each corner of each large cross stitch is again crossed, this time with small stitches taken

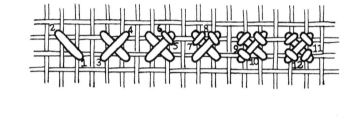

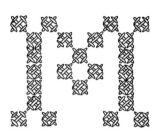

Letter M *in crossed corners stitch*

at right angles to the original cross. The stitch can be worked all at once, or by doing the small stitches (perhaps in a contrasting color) after all the large crosses are completed.

herringbone stitch

Herringbone stitch is actually a continuous line of interlaced cross stitches with the crossings off-center. It can be used to fill shapes, but looks best when used in a long band. It can be worked spaced far apart, or close

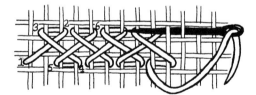

together, tall or short. But, whatever way is chosen, the stitches must be kept regular, with all the diagonals parallel, for a neat appearance. The reverse side of the work forms a series of neat backstitches when worked close together.

four-sided line stitch

Four-sided line stitch is often used for working alphabets. In some early historic samplers entire patterns are seen worked in this stitch instead of cross stitch. When the four-sided stitch is used, a very delicate and lacy appearance is given to the work. Any pattern indicated by lines rather than filled shapes can be done, such as the borders numbered 9, 12, 13, 15, 16, and 18 on Chart IV.

The stitch is not at all complicated, and only four or five squares need be done on a little scrap to get the rhythm. Remembering that the front forms a little box, while the back shows a cross stitch with one of the arms crossed twice, will make working it easier.

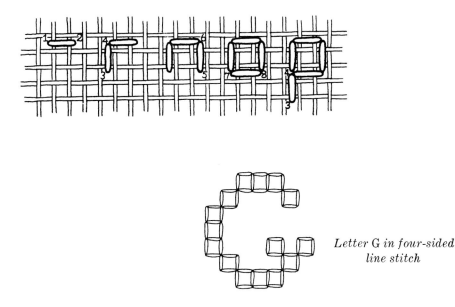

Letter G in four-sided
line stitch

Bring the needle out at 1 and in two threads to the right at 2. Cross under diagonally and bring the needle out again two threads under 1, at 3, then in two threads above at 4. Continue by following the diagrams until you have completed one square. It can be seen that stitch 7-8 has already formed the stitch 1-2 for the next square, so go right to stitch 3-4.

satin stitch and variations

Satin stitch is one of the stitches most frequently seen on historic samplers. It is probably the second embroidery stitch a child learns, but is one of the most difficult to accomplish perfectly. The problem lies in the length of the stitch. The longer it gets, the more prone it is to an untidy appearance. The thread used must be just the right thickness or the stitch will look either skimpy or crowded.

The thread is carried across the shape to be filled, inserted into the material and brought out again just next to the starting point of the previous stitch. It may be brought out higher or lower than the previous stitch, but must lie right next to it. Evenness in placing the stitches is made easier by the use of counted-thread fabric. An embroidery hoop or frame will keep the stitches from puckering the fabric, always a problem with any long embroidery stitch. The illustration shows satin stitches worked over a different number of horizontal threads.

Letter E *in satin stitch*

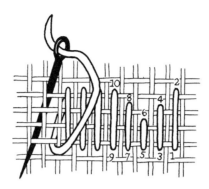

A change in direction of the slant of each group of satin stitches adds dimension and a slight amount of shading. The illustration shows a leaf or petal shape done in satin stitch worked in a different direction on either side of the center.

For less abrupt shading, encroaching satin stitch should be used. Here the first line of satin stitches is worked as usual. The second row is worked from the bottom up so that the needle can be inserted between the bases of the stitches in the previous row.

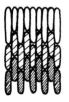

For even more subtle shading, long and short stitch should be used. For this stitch work a row of alternating long and short satin stitches left to right along the outer edge of the design, bringing the needle out at the top, and in again at the bottom. Work the next row from right to left, this time making all the stitches as long as the short stitches in the first row, and bringing the needle out at the bottom, in again at the top. The next row is worked left to right again, also bringing the needle out at the bottom and in at the top, with uniformly long stitches. As can be seen from the illustration, the last row to be filled leaves short spaces which must be filled with stitches half the length of the short stitches. When working long and short stitch from a curved line, proceed as usual, but slant the outer stitches toward the center. As your rows progress you will have to use fewer stitches in each row, but continue staggering the stitches as best you can.

tent stitch

After cross and satin stitch, tent stitch is probably the most universally known. It can be used any place cross stitch is used since it is basically half a cross stitch, although the thread will have to be made thicker to cover the fabric. Since it looks like half a cross stitch, it takes half the time to work and is very useful for filling large areas of color. Its only drawback in terms of design is that identical motifs on two sides of a center line will not look perfectly symmetrical. The reason for this is that no matter which method is used in its working, the stitch always slants from bottom left to top right. The illustration shows that lines slanting up to the right will be continuous, while lines slanting up to the left will be broken by other colors or background fabric.

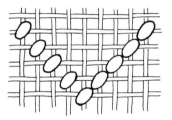

When worked in straight lines (top to bottom or right to left), tent stitch is called continental stitch. It should be used for long lines and for outlining large areas of color, which will then be filled in with tent stitch worked diagonally, called basket weave stitch. Notice that continental stitch will show a longer, more diagonal stitch on the back than on the front.

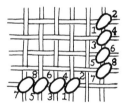

Continental stitch is started at the lower right and worked toward the left or at the top right and worked down. When one row is completed, turn the work upside down and stitch the next row, working in the same direction as you did in the first row: that is, toward the left or toward the bottom.

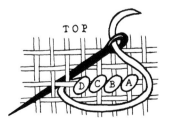

Tent stitch worked diagonally is called basket weave. Since it pulls the fabric out of shape less than continental stitch, it should be used rather than the latter wherever possible.

Basket weave stitch is worked starting at the top right hand corner by adding more stitches in each diagonal row as it is worked. When working downward the needle is held vertically; when working upward the needle is held horizontally. This produces a pattern on the back which gives the stitch its name. Whether working up or down, the needle goes under 2 fabric threads and emerges in an empty hole. There is no need to turn the work when starting another row.

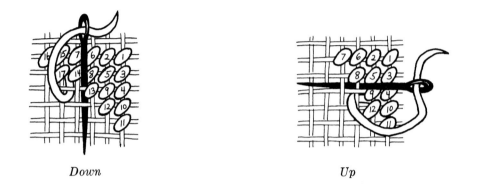

Down   *Up*

If two up rows or two down rows are worked in succession, a ridge will show on the front of the work. This can be avoided by always ending a thread in the middle of a row. This way, when the work is picked up again, you will know in which direction to start stitching.

mosaic stitch

Mosiac stitch, although not seen frequently on historic samplers, is a useful stitch for filling in color areas and for lettering. It is made of 2 small tent stitches with 1 larger one between them. Together they make

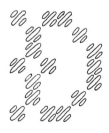

Letter D *in mosaic stitch*

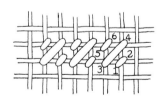

a neat little square covering 2 fabric threads each way. It may be enlarged to cover 3 fabric threads by adding an even longer tent stitch in the center.

stem stitch

Stem stitch is used most often to make curving vines or stems in conjunction with satin-stitch flowers on embroidery not necessarily dependent on countable threads. When neatly worked, it resembles a twisted cord.

Stem stitch and backstitch are the exact opposites of each other. Stem stitch is worked to the right, backstitch to the left. Stem stitch leaves a long overlapping stitch on the front and short straight stitches on the back, while backstitch leaves short straight stitches on the front and long overlapping stitches on the back.

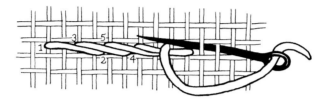

Work stem stitch from left to right. Bring the needle out at 1, in again at 2 which is four threads to the right. For the next stitch bring the needle out again two threads back at 3, and back in again four threads ahead at 4. Always keep your thread either above or below the needle for each line of stitching. A change in the position of the thread will reverse the spiral effect of the stitch and this would be quite visible in the middle of a row.

backstitch

Backstitch is useful for indicating details in motifs already filled in with cross or satin stitch, and depends on regularity for its effectiveness.

Work from right to left. Bring the needle out at 1, in at 2, which is two threads to the right. For the next stitch bring the needle out again four threads ahead at 3, and back in at 4, which is two threads back and at the same place where the previous stitch emerged.

eyelet stitch, algerian-eye, or star stitch

Eyelet stitch is a decorative stitch which leaves small holes in the fabric. It is found on historic samplers, used mainly for narrow horizontal borders done in a single line or alternately spaced in double lines, and for complete alphabets. It is actually a series of 8 stitches, each one over 2 threads going into the same center hole. The completed stitch covers a square 4 threads wide in each direction.

Letter J in eyelet stitch

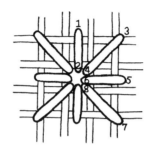

Starting with a straight vertical stitch, complete the unit, working clockwise, by making 7 other stitches, each going back into the center hole. Pull each separate stitch tight for a large hole. When each complete stitch is finished, run your working thread through the threads on the back to secure it, making sure the eyelet hole is not covered as you move on to the next stitch.

attached fly stitch

This stitch was used in historic samplers for stitching willow and poplar trees (as seen in the schoolhouse sampler in plate IX), for in one stitch both the branch and leaves could be indicated. It was also used for vines encircling floral motifs or lettering. Three methods of working the stitch

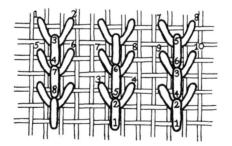

follow. They may all be worked over 4 threads instead of the 2 illustrated and may be worked in curved, horizontal, or diagonal lines as well. In all three methods the wings of the fly do not pierce the fabric as they pass under the straight body.

The traditional method of working the stitch is on the left. First take a loose horizontal stitch over 2 threads. Bring your needle out again in the center, 1 thread down, pulling the loose first stitch below the needle. Reinsert the needle 2 threads down to anchor the horizontal stitch in a "V" shape. For the second stitch the needle emerges 2 threads below the start of the first horizontal stitch.

Since working in the traditional way necessitates working from the tip of the branch inward to the trunk—and this is a cumbersome way of designing a graceful tree limb—, a different method has been devised which is not evident on the sampler surface. This method, seen in the center, is to work the stitch backwards, making the anchoring vertical stitch first, then bringing the thread out to the left and above, looping it under the anchor stitch without going through the material, then going through the fabric at the top right. In this way a symmetrically balanced and graceful tree can be easily formed with free-hand stitching.

Another way, seen on the right, would be to work only the anchoring stitches along the entire limb first, doing them in backstitch, later going back to fill in the loops which indicate the leaves. By this method the limb and leaves may be of different colors, dark green or brown for the limb, light green or yellow-green for the leaves.

rococo stitch

Rococo stitch is rarely seen in modern needlework, but can be found quite often on historic samplers depicting strawberries, and sometimes flowers or geometric motifs. The little horizontal stitches, indicating seeds, which tie down the longer vertical stitches, and the way the diamond-shaped clusters can be put together, make it the obvious choice for stitching the strawberry. Notice that it cannot be charted in the usual way, as for cross stitch.

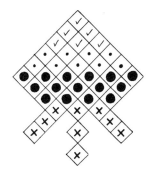

*Chart for a
strawberry using a
rococo stitch*

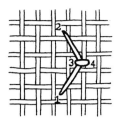 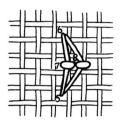

 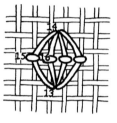

It seems quite intricate, but is really easy if you follow both the illustrations and the written directions, although fitting so many stitches into so small a space makes it a little tedious to work. You may have to use a lighter weight thread than you would for cross stitch on the same fabric because ten threads must pierce one hole.

Take a loose vertical stitch upward over 4 threads and bring your needle out 2 horizontal threads down and 1 to the right, keeping the vertical stitch to the right of the needle. Tie the vertical stitch down with a short stitch taken over 1 vertical thread, 2 threads to the right. Now bring your needle out again at the same place it first emerged and make another vertical stitch into the same hole as the first one, but this time tie it down only 1 thread to the right. The third vertical stitch will be tied down 1 thread to the left, the fourth will be tied down 2 threads to the left. Pull each stitch tightly to make the little holes indicative of the stitch. When the stitches are clustered together 10 threads will go through one hole in the fabric, so it should be obvious why holes are formed. The stitch clusters may be worked horizontally or diagonally. Remember to keep your thread to the right of the needle when working, and work each cluster from the right to the left.

✖

WORKING THE SAMPLER

✖

preparation

Having chosen and graphed your design, and chosen your threads and fabric, you are almost ready to stitch your sampler. Fabric as it is brought home from the store is ready for stitching. No prewashing or any other special treatment is necessary. All that is required is to cut it to the proper size and put in a narrow hem all the way around. To cut your sampler to the proper size, first determine that size from the chart you have prepared. Plan on having at least 6″ more fabric in each dimension. For example, if your sampler is to be 20″ x 30″, cut your fabric to measure no less than 26″ x 36″. This extra fabric allows for a small hem to prevent the edges from fraying while you are working the sampler, 1½″ of unworked fabric to place inside the frame, and the rest to tack on the back of your mounting board. More than 6″ can be allowed, but less than 6″ would mean that the mounting would have to be worked quite close to the sampler itself. Historic samplers sometimes were cut and hemmed to within ½″ of the outside stitching, and mounting them today can pose a problem because of the lack of extra material.

Put in a narrow hem all around the fabric by either hand-rolling, binding with tape (either masking tape folded over the edge, or pre-folded bias tape sewn on), or by using the zig-zag stitch on your sewing machine. You could, if you wish, put your hem in with your embroidery thread, by first pulling a fabric thread on all four sides and using a decorative stitch such as herringbone. This fancy hemming could also be done after the sampler is finished, using a temporary hem beforehand.

Of course before you stitch, you will have to cut your thread to needle length. This measurement differs from thread to thread. Some threads fray easily, some do not. Experiment with yours to determine the proper working length. When the cut end shows signs of fraying, the thread is too long and you will wind up wasting a great deal of thread rather than saving thread. The general rule for cutting threads to working length is that for fabrics with high thread counts the thread should be shorter than for fabrics with low thread counts. The more times a thread is pulled through the fabric the more apt it is to fray.

To start your thread in the work, do not knot it because, when your sampler is finally mounted, any overly thick area on the back of the work will show up as a lump on the front. Always run your new thread through the stitches on the back of the sampler for about an inch to anchor it. To be absolutely sure that it will not pull out, run the thread through the stitches on the back in two directions; that is, run your thread away from the starting place and then double back to it. To start the very first thread on the sampler, leave a long end of thread on the front of the work. When you have finished working that thread, pull the end through to the back, thread it into the needle, and run it through the stitches on the back as for any other thread. To end a thread, run it through the stitches on the back the same way.

Sometimes while working you will find that your yarn or thread has become quite twisted. In that case just drop the threaded needle so that it hangs straight down and let it unwind on its own. To prevent the thread from twisting in the first place, many embroiderers simply twirl the needle in their fingers every other stitch or so.

We all make mistakes, and, when that happens, stitches must be ripped out. This is where that sharp-pointed pair of scissors in your work-basket comes in handy. Carefully slip one blade under one stitch thread showing on the back of the work and clip it. Do this every few stitches, being very careful not to clip the fabric as well. Then with your needle or a pair of tweezers, pull the unwanted stitches out. Do not try to reuse a thread that has been taken out of your sampler. Of course, if only one or two stitches have been misplaced, simply unthread the needle, pull out half of each unwanted cross stitch at a time, re-thread the needle, and continue stitching.

It is possible when working on fabric with a very high thread count to carry a working thread across the back from one color area to the next. It is wise not to make this jump too long, for the loose thread on the back is apt to snag and pull. If you must make a long jump, try to catch the thread under the backs of a few stitches along the way. On fabric of low thread count, where the holes between the threads are fairly large, do not skip from color area to color area, because the long threads might show through on the front. Some Victorian samplers worked on double-mesh canvas which do not have their backgrounds filled in are good examples of this sloppy workmanship.

stitching

To start, fold your fabric in half lengthwise (it is traditional when working on embroidery fabric to have the selvages on either side and the cut edges at the top and bottom), and mark a spot on the fold 3″ from the top. A straight pin will do for marking. Assuming that your sampler will have a border, find the center top stitch on the graphed border, for this is where you will start stitching at the pin mark.

Most borders from historic samplers are based on an undulating line which encloses alternatively placed flowers or berries. To make working a border much easier, and to save yourself endless counting of diagonal lines of stitches, work 1 repeat in the undulating line of the border, then sew 2 rows of guideline stitches the full length of that border line, at the outer and inner edges of the diagonal lines. Then, as you complete that line of border, the only counting you will have to do will be in the straight lines of stitches. Turn your corner, work another repeat, run another 2 rows of guideline threads and continue the border. Do this on all four sides. Of course the guideline threads are easily pulled out when the border is done.

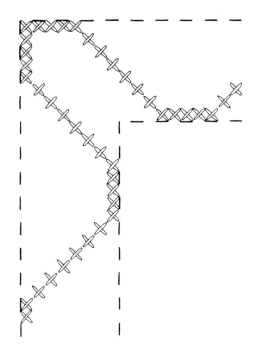

Putting in guideline threads is not necessary, but they can be real timesavers when working any type of counted-thread embroidery. They should be done in a light sewing thread, the kind used for hemming and machine stitching, and should be run through the material in a regular pattern, under 2 threads and over 2 threads. This can be done much like weaving, running the needle through a number of fabric threads before bringing it out and starting again. Running the thread under 2 and over 2 makes it much easier to count stitches and spaces as well. When all your cross stitching is completed the guideline threads can easily be pulled out.

Guideline threads are also useful when you are trying to line up two motifs symmetrically on opposite sides of the sampler, as in the Pennsylvania-German sampler in plate VII. In all samplers it is useful to run a row of guideline stitching straight down the center, from top to bottom, and you may find other places where guidelines can be of help in your particular sampler.

When you are done with the undulating line of the border, if you have counted correctly you should have about 3″ to the edge of your fabric on all four sides.

It is now advisable to leave the rest of the border until last, since handling in working the interior elements of the sampler tends to rough up the stitches on the outer edges. But if you are like most embroiderers, you will not be able to leave the border before working at least one complete repeat to see how the colors and design will look; so satisfy your curiosity, but no more.

If the interior of your sampler is made up mostly of horizontal motifs, start with the one at the top and work it completely, stitching from the center outward toward either edge. Then stitch the one below it in the same manner. Proceed this way until you have reached the place where your signature will be, skip that (in most cases it will be the last horizontal row), and finish the sampler by working the rest of the outer border, and then working your signature.

If the interior of your sampler is divided into two parts, the lower section will probably have an important pictorial scene while the upper section will have smaller motifs or lettering. Do the upper section first. After working the lower section, complete the outer border and then sign your sampler.

If the interior of your sampler is made up mostly of scattered motifs, start either at the top center or bottom center and work outward toward the motifs that fall next to, below, or above each other. Whether you start at the top or bottom depends only on how accessible the center motif at each place is. We started at the top of the Pennsylvania-German sampler because the center carnation motif had an empty space running down the center line and was therefore easy to place. Complete the outer border if there is one, and then sign your sampler.

In most samplers, wherever it seems easiest and most logical to place the first stitches correctly is a fine place to start.

In all cases it is wise to leave all large areas of satin stitch until last, even until after you complete your signature. Otherwise they may be roughed up while you are working other elements of the sampler.

Remove the guideline threads and your sampler is finished.

washing, pressing, and blocking

Friends tell tales of grandmothers who worked their embroidery wearing gloves, and who covered completed areas with pillow cases, so as not to soil their work. You could go to those extremes, but you probably would not enjoy picking up your needle for very long. If you are careful and work with clean hands, if you do not carry a cup of coffee over your work to your lips, your sampler may look rumpled but will not become terribly soiled. If it looks as if it could use some cleaning, try a cold water bath first, then, if necessary, a solution of mild soap like Woolite or Ivory and lukewarm water. Dunk it, or swish it around, or knead it, but do not scrub. Rinse thoroughly in cool water. Never wring, but roll the embroidery in a thirsty towel, changing to a dry one when the first gets too wet. Spread the sampler flat to dry (but not in the sun) or press immediately while it is still damp.

To press, lay a single thickness of towel on your ironing board. Put your sampler on the towel with the right side down. Then dampen the sampler if necessary with either a clean sponge or spray bottle, and iron lightly on the wrong side with a dry iron. Do not use a steam iron since they sometimes spit and can leave stains. Be sure to use the proper setting on your iron for the fabric on which your sampler is worked. A preliminary test on a small scrap for proper heat-setting would be wise.

Samplers worked in wool and using large amounts of tent stitch, like the schoolhouse sampler (plate IX) need blocking rather than pressing. Tent stitch tends to pull the fabric out of shape, even when it is worked diagonally (basket weave stitch).

To block, use a soft board (plywood is good), larger all around than your entire piece of fabric. Cover the board with brown paper upon which you have drawn an outline of the outer dimensions of the fabric, indicating the center of each line. Mark the center of each edge of the sampler, and lay it face down on the paper. Using tacks that will not rust, and spacing them about ½″ apart, stretch the sampler firmly to fit the drawn outline. First tack the top edge, making sure that the corners and centers line up with the marks on the paper. Continue in this manner, doing the left edge, then the bottom, then the right edge. When the sampler is completely tacked down, saturate the entire surface with water. If you wet just the worked areas, the fabric may be watermarked when it is dry. Use a clean sponge or a spray bottle. Soak up the excess water with a towel and set the board aside to dry for a day out of the sun. When dry, remove the tacks and your sampler should be squared up, the stitches standing out boldly, and the sampler ready for mounting.

mounting

Cut a piece of ¼″-thick standard Masonite or plywood to the dimensions of the worked area of your sampler, plus at least ¾″ on all four sides. The extra is to allow a small area of unworked border inside the frame, plus ½″ that the frame will overlap.

Cut a piece of prewashed (to remove any possible chemical sizing), unbleached muslin at least 2″ bigger all around than the board. Using a mixture of white glue and water in equal amounts, or textile glue, paint the top surface of the board and then lay the muslin on it. Smooth the muslin with your hands so that it lies flat and tight. There should be just enough glue on the board so that the muslin does not feel wet and no glue seeps through. Turn the board over and apply glue to its outer edges. Then, pulling tightly, glue the protruding edges of the muslin in place, cutting away excess fabric on a diagonal so that no fabric lies on top of another piece of fabric. Allow this to dry thoroughly, at least overnight.

To be absolutely sure that nothing harmful can reach your sampler, a sheet of acid-free, 100-percent rag parchment paper or cardboard can be laid over the muslin-covered board just before actually mounting the sampler. This paper is available at most framing stores.

The next step is to insure a perfectly mounted sampler and involves a bit more work, but the finished product is worth every bit of extra effort. Lay your sampler on the completely dry board, making sure it is centered. Pin the fabric to the narrow edge of the board with eight push pins, one an inch away from each corner. Then, after finding the fabric thread on each of the four sides which will run along the exact center of the narrow edge of the board (by counting threads if necessary), remove the sampler from the board and mark that thread all the way around the sampler by running a light sewing thread through the material. Replace the sampler on the board and pin in place in the narrow edge of Masonite or plywood through that thread, pinning every inch or less. Now turn the board over so that the wrong side is up. Fold and miter the corners neatly, as you would in making a hospital corner on a bed, and stitch them in place by hand. Use masking tape or push pins to hold them in place temporarily.

At this point there are two methods that can be used to affix the sampler permanently to the board. The traditional method is to lace it on the edges with long stitches, first from side to side, then from top to bottom, using carpet and button-hole thread or crochet cotton and pulling tightly to keep the fabric firmly stretched.

The second method, used on the new samplers in this book, has proved quite satisfactory. Using a staple gun and ¼" staples, pull the fabric taut and insert a staple every ½" at the very edge of the fabric all the way around. Remove the push pins and you have a sampler mounted with not one crooked thread. The staples lie flat, do not pull holes in the fabric the way lacing tends to (although lacing through a piece of muslin or linen sewn to the sampler edges eliminates holes in the sampler itself), hold the sampler securely in place, and yet can be pried out easily if for any reason the sampler is to be removed from the board.

3

A GARLAND
OF MOTIFS

The following section contains motifs and designs which were for the most part counted out stitch by stitch from historic samplers. We are offering these as a guide for modern embroiderers who wish to stitch samplers using traditional motifs. Many are as satisfactory today as when they were first designed. Geometric motifs and designs drawn from nature are timeless and can be used unchanged in any age. Buildings from the last two centuries of the types depicted on samplers still stand and are used, loved, and lived in. Of all the individual designs given here, only the clothing on the human figures is dated. If you wish, it would be a simple matter to modernize their dress.

The traditional sampler stitch is cross stitch, but the designs can be worked in a number of other counted-thread stitches. Just be careful that the stitch you choose is in the same scale as cross stitch—that is, that it covers the same square of four threads. Otherwise the dimensions of the entire sampler will be changed.

You may also want to do some designs in satin stitch. Historic samplers using large areas of satin stitch were done on closely woven linen or satin, with fine silk thread. Heavier weight thread on the more loosely woven fabric available today may be used by the modern embroiderer, but remember that the designs may look cruder and coarser than the originals. Of course, this may be a desired effect.

After designs have been worked in cross stitch or satin stitch, certain detail may be added by re-embroidering in back stitch or stem stitch, right over the preliminary stitching. Such things as facial features, folds or designs in skirts and jackets, and paneling on doors can be successfully stitched over flat color areas.

The color symbols on the charts indicate general color families. With the hundreds of threads and fabrics available to the modern embroiderer it would have been too limiting to specify particular shades. It also would have denied modern embroiderers the delight of creating totally individual and unique pieces of needlework. Many of the types of threads and fabrics available today have been described in chapter 2.

The pages of charted motifs and designs are marked with color symbols with each separate symbol standing for a single stitch in that color.

Master Color Key

●	red		—	middle green
·	middle red, flesh, peach		Z	light green
√	pale pink, ecru		⌞·	dark blue
=	dark brown		O	medium blue
+	brown		⌞	light blue
□	tan		P	purple, lavender, fuschia
⊓	orange		■	black
V	yellow		△	grey
X	green, dark or bright		/	white

*Each separate color symbol in each separate square on the graph
is to be interpreted as one cross stitch in that color.
Color areas which are outlined are to be done in satin stitch.*

A word about choosing your colors is necessary, for here more than anywhere else is where you decide the overall feeling of your sampler. Looking at historic samplers, you see for the most part soft, pale, almost faded-looking colors. Remember that those colors were probably bright and clear when the samplers were done 100 to 300 years ago. Samplers that were never framed but were rolled up and tucked away in a drawer immediately after working, and the reverse side of framed samplers, reveal bright colors that have not faded through long exposure to sunlight or fluorescent light. Instead of trying to make your sampler into an exact reproduction of an historic sampler, you can choose soft colors that show your work to be a modern adaptation. On the other hand, you can choose bright, clear colors for a sampler that will be an obvious example of modern needlework utilizing traditional motifs. For instance, when looking for a family of greens you could choose between soft olives or bright kellys. With reds choose between rose-brown shades or clear cardinals. Both methods can be quite successful.

Don't be afraid to change colors, add details, and put the motifs together in any way you wish to make your own unique sampler. Think of adding bright things like sequins for buttons down the front of a man's coat, beads for the eyes of birds, and even specialty threads for certain highlights. Add stripes, bows, and shadows on voluminous skirts, lattice and vines on houses, or four shades of a color where only three are indicated. In other words, feel free to make these designs totally your own.

Chart I is framed by two spiral columns topped by curving arches. These were adapted from samplers done by students at Miss Polly Balch's school in Providence, Rhode Island, near the end of the eighteenth century. To fit the space available on your sampler, they could easily be lengthened or widened. Instead of an alphabet, a family record or a depiction of a pastoral scene could be set between them. The alphabet charted between the columns was used almost exclusively by the Quaker schools, principally in Pennsylvania, and can be found on many of their distinctive samplers. This pairing of columns and alphabet is a perfect example of the compatibility of traditional motifs. Although these motifs came from totally different cultures, they appear on the page as if they were designed specifically for each other.

Chart II consists of two capital alphabets and two lower-case alphabets, plus one line of numbers. These two alphabets, with slight variations in certain letters (particularly in *m, n, h,* and *x*) appear in almost every sampler which includes lettering, both European and American. The first alphabet, being the smallest, is seen most frequently because, with its use, more lettering can be fitted into small spaces. It is also seen many times on single samplers done in various stitches besides cross stitch. It lends itself admirably to crossed corners stitch, eyelet stitch, satin stitch, mosaic stitch, and four-sided line stitch.

Charts I and II have been designed so that with the addition of a simple border and signature and perhaps a small geometric motif on either side of the numbers in Chart II, they can be stitched directly as complete samplers. They would present no great difficulty to a child doing a first piece of embroidery.

Charts III through VI offer 33 graphed border designs already cornered for you. They may be personalized in many ways. Following are just some of many possibilities. Border #2 can have the diamond shapes outlined in cross stitch, then filled in with satin stitch. The flowers in border #4 may be done totally in satin stitch. The circular shapes in border #16 can be done in alternating colors and linked together, or they could be made into solid and overlapping circles in alternating colors. The tendrils emanating from the flower heads in border #18 could be done in back stitch, and the rest of the design in four-sided line stitch. The acorns in border #20 could be done in satin stitch in two shades of brown or turned into strawberries by the use of two shades of red. The solid black line in border #26 could become a checkered line.

Chart VII and the lowest motif on Chart VIII show how flowers were usually depicted. For the most part they were not realistic, the Pennsylvania-German examples being quite abstract. The lower-left and lower-right examples on Chart VII and the bottom example on Chart VIII are typically Pennsylvania-German. The two center flowers on Chart VIII and the wreath above them were taken from samplers of the nineteenth century and are typical of designs done in Berlin work using wool on canvas. The two flowers were charted from the sampler seen in color plate IV. Such designs for realistically portrayed flowers can be found in profusion today in instructions for needlepoint. Use the wreath to enclose a name or date.

Although flower borders and sprays were often done completely in satin stitch on historic samplers, designs of that type are not given in this book. Should you want to work such designs, numerous patterns can be found in instructional books for crewelwork and free embroidery. If you decide to work such a border, remember that large areas of satin stitch should be confined to the finer mesh fabrics since the typically smooth

�֍ *A Garland of Motifs* ✗

85

and glossy surface and regular outlines of satin stitch tend to look coarse and even skimpy (if the thread is too fine) on the larger mesh fabrics.

Charts IX and X show some of the variety of trees found on historic samplers. The two trees at the bottom of Chart IX were taken from the same sampler. They are basically the same tree, the one on the right having the tiers placed upside-down. They were originally placed alternately in a long row climbing to the top of a hill. Any of these trees can be made taller by adding more tiers. This will make them wider as well. The tree at the top right of Chart IX can be turned into a tall poplar by adding more rows to the middle unchanging section. The weeping willow tree at the bottom left of Chart X can be turned into a weeping cherry by doing the pendant branches in pink, into a wisteria by doing them in lavender.

Charts XI and XII include some of the myriad birds and beasts found on American samplers. The American eagle is not frequently seen but is included here because the samplers that do feature it are historically very important. Small birds like doves or lovebirds are quite often found facing each other, bill to bill, like the two birds on Chart XI, third from the bottom left. Refer to page 57 for more information about some of the animals presented in Chart XII, and the large building in Chart XIII.

Charts XIV and XV show four more buildings, both public and private. Those on Chart XIV are shown completely frontally; those on Chart XV are shown in the naive, mechanical perspective so often found on historic samplers and other folk art. It depicts both the front and side view of the same building in frontal view, instead of the more advanced and difficult perspective of three-quarter view. This distorted perspective is literally imposed by the limitations of the cross stitchery itself, which make it nearly impossible to stitch successfully any angle but one of 45° and even more difficult to stitch a subtle curve.

On the larger buildings on all three charts bricks may be indicated by the addition of a grid of white lines, much as was done on the foundation of the house in Chart XIII.

One method of working shutters on buildings, other than working them in cross stitch, is to do them in long vertical satin stitches, anchoring those down with a few horizontal satin stitches at the two places that divide the shutters into thirds.

The little boy in the family in Chart XVI is missing in the original sampler from which the group was adapted. Here he is added easily, using the same relative size as the little girl, and the same clothing as his father. The difference between the clothing on the father and son is a perfect example of the necessity of deleting details when charting designs for cross stitch. Here, the son loses the bright vest that is visible under his father's coat.

The man and woman facing the urn in Chart XVIII come from a mourning picture, which, strictly speaking, is not a sampler but more of a needlework painting. The monument itself can just be outlined in back-stitch or filled in with cross or satin stitch. Inside the round and oval medallions were placed inscriptions honoring a departed family member or national hero. The original inscriptions on this mourning picture include "The loss ever shall we mourn" in the oval medallion and "Sacred to the memory of the illustrious Washington" in the round medallion. A small picture of the departed was sometimes inserted in the medallion on the urn. These inscriptions can be done in cross stitch over a single thread, written directly on paper which is then glued to the fabric, or painted on the fabric itself, which in the originals was usually satin. An alternative method would be to paint the inscription on satin and apply the satin to the linen sampler with tiny stitches. Some mourning pictures can be found which were done on linen in cross stitch, which is why these figures are included here.

If all these human figures are executed in satin stitch, there will be no difficulty in defining forms that cross each other when they are done in the same color. All that is needed is to slant the direction of the satin stitch in the crossing form in a different direction from the form underneath. If you work them as charted in cross stitch, notice that a line in the chart indicates where small straight stitches (backstitch) in either the same, darker, or contrasting color can be used to add definition.

Chart XIX contains some miscellaneous motifs. The castle or church-like design is seen in some variations, mostly on European samplers, but can be found on some American samplers done by girls of German or Dutch descent. A few changes can bring imaginative results: by eliminating the center door section and replacing it with a tied-back drapery framing a small figure, it becomes a puppet theatre; by standing birds on the towers and on a pole-supported platform in front, it becomes a grand birdhouse.

The cornucopia is from nineteenth-century Berlin work and can be filled with sprays of natural-looking flowers. Although most cornucopiae are found with the opening downward, this one was originally seen as presented (see color plate IV), almost as though it was the handle of a large bouquet. When filled with flowers, it should be thought of as the central motif of a sampler because of its size.

Another design usually seen as a central motif is the hexagonal medallion with facing birds inside at the top and bottom. Between the pairs of birds, in cross stitch worked over a single thread, are the phrases, "An emblem of love," or "An emblem of innocence."

As chart I illustrates, most classic motifs from different cultures and different eras can be successfully combined in modern samplers. On the other hand, realistic and highly abstract figures may clash. The naturalistic flowers on Chart VIII would look out of place if combined with the Pennsylvania-German flowers on the same chart. Any of the more stylized and abstract motifs can be used together, as can the more naturalistic motifs, but the two different styles should not be mixed on the same sampler.

Although this collection of motifs from historic American samplers is extensive, it is by no means complete. As new samplers come to light from private homes, new motifs continually appear, some just variations on motifs already noted but others completely original and never seen before. As you become more adept at charting designs yourself, you will also find, as we did, motifs from sources other than historic samplers that can be adapted to this form of needlework.

I

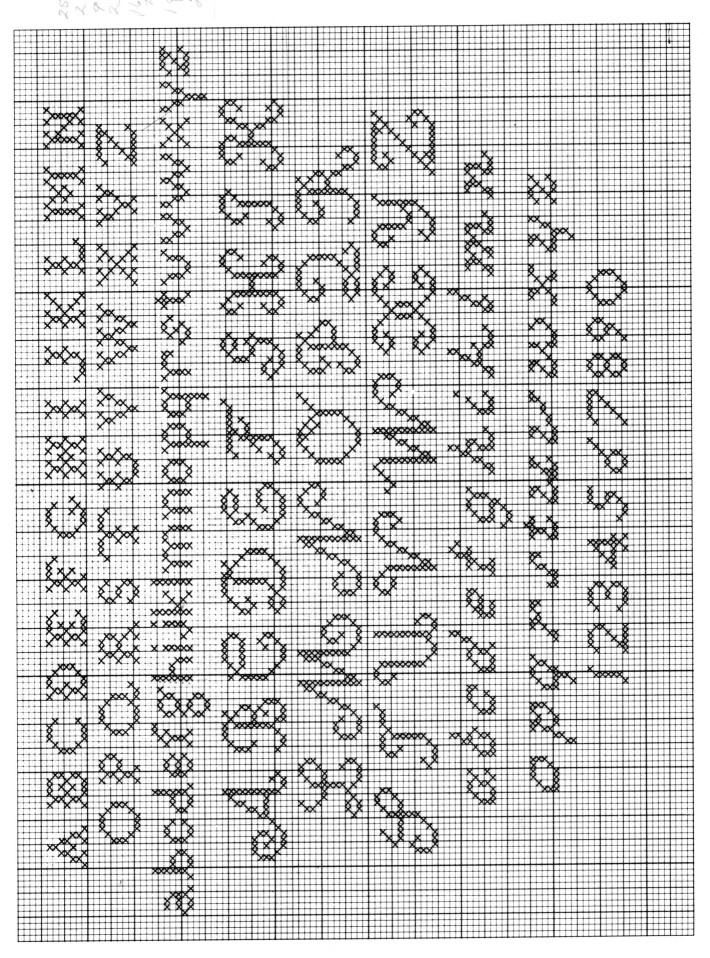

II

33

200

1   2   3   4   5   6   7   8

III

ak blue   red ⦿ P   white

9   10   11   12   13   14   15   16   17   18

IV

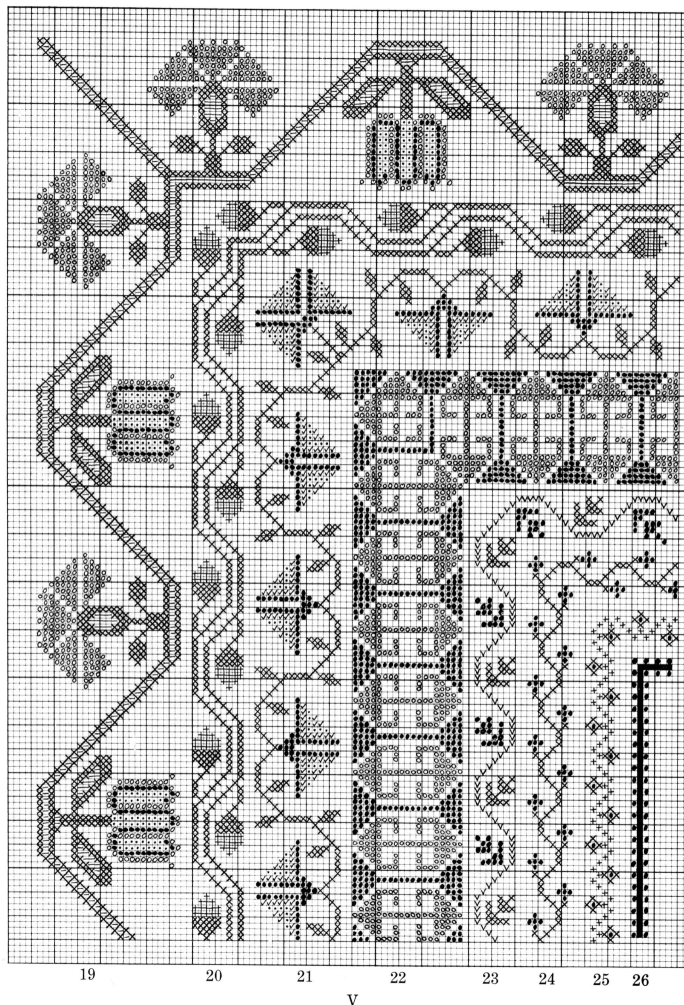

VII

VIII

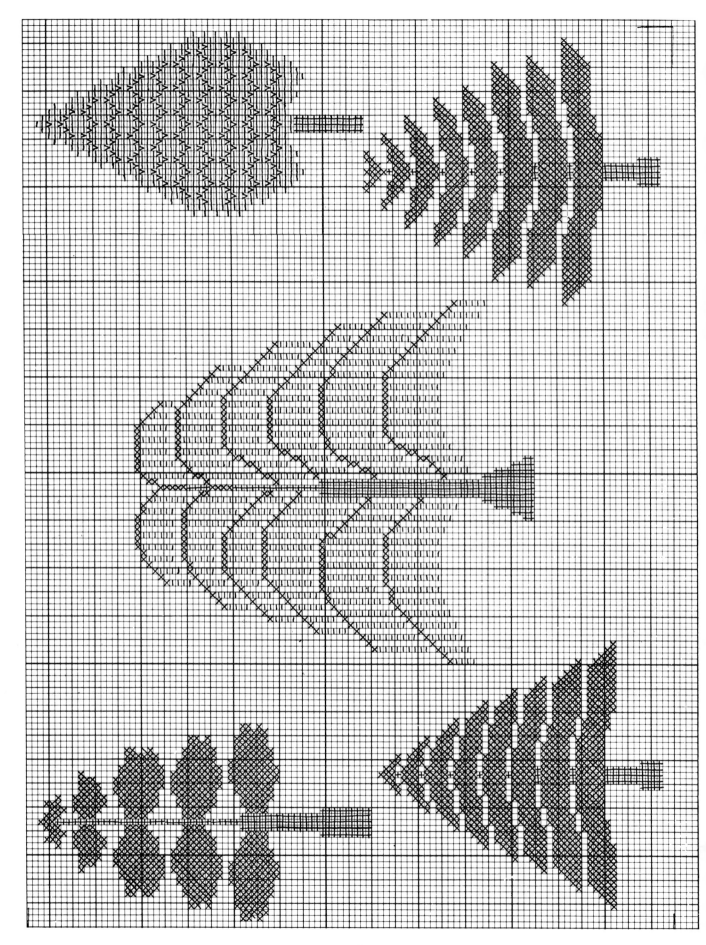

IX

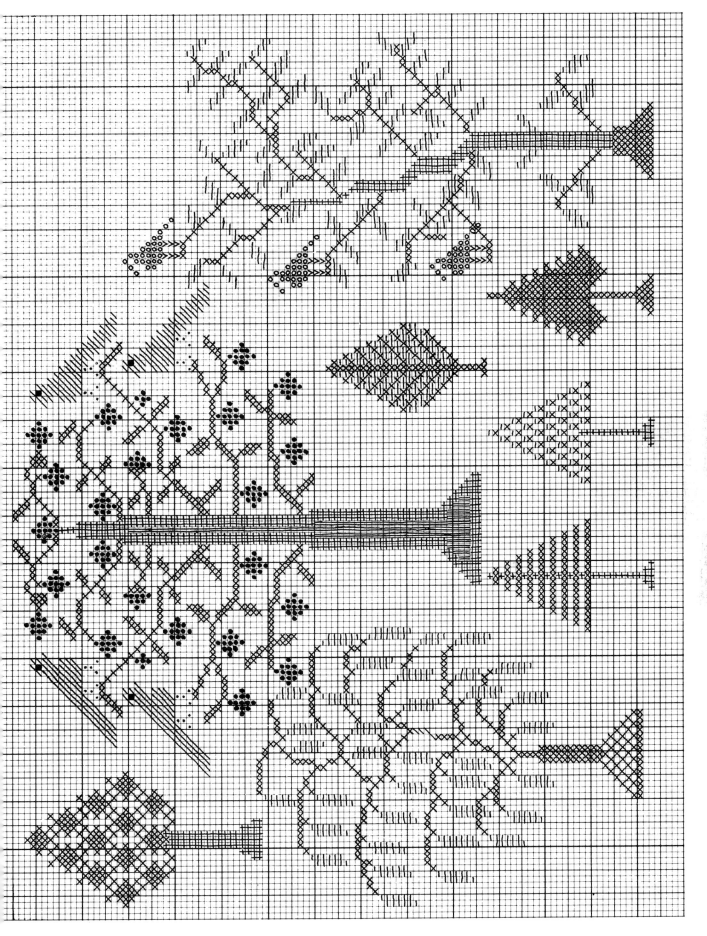

X

XI

XII

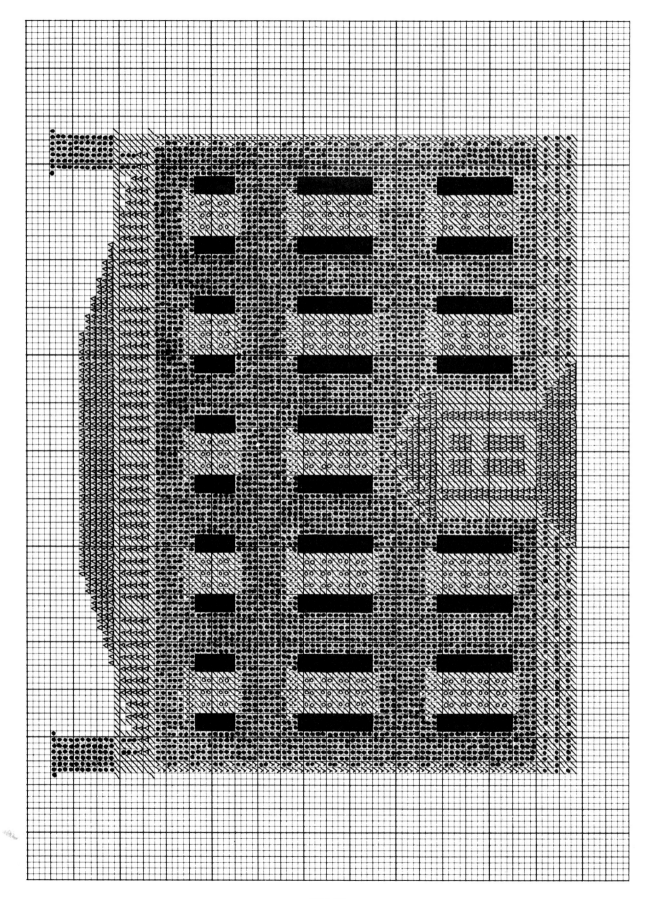

XIII

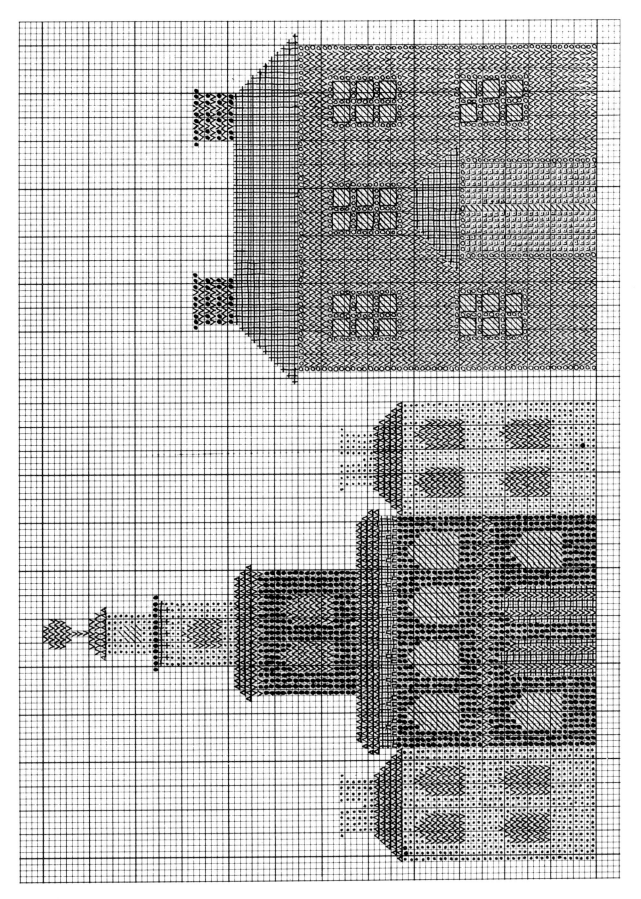

XIV

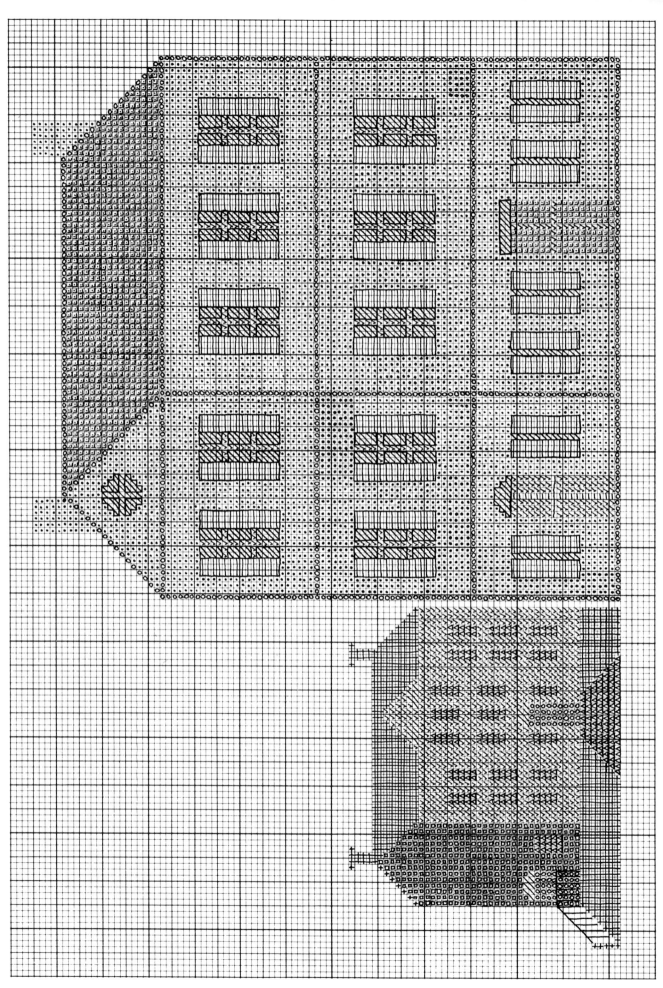

XV

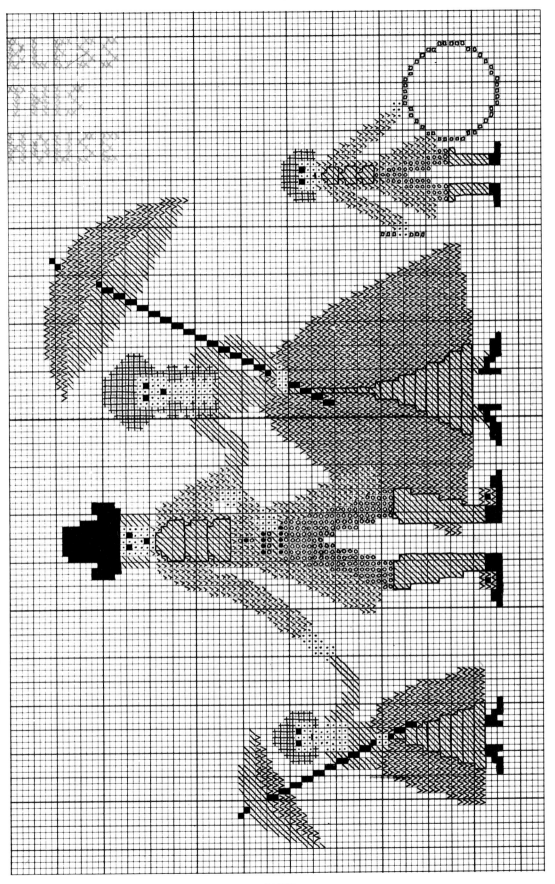

XVI

XVII

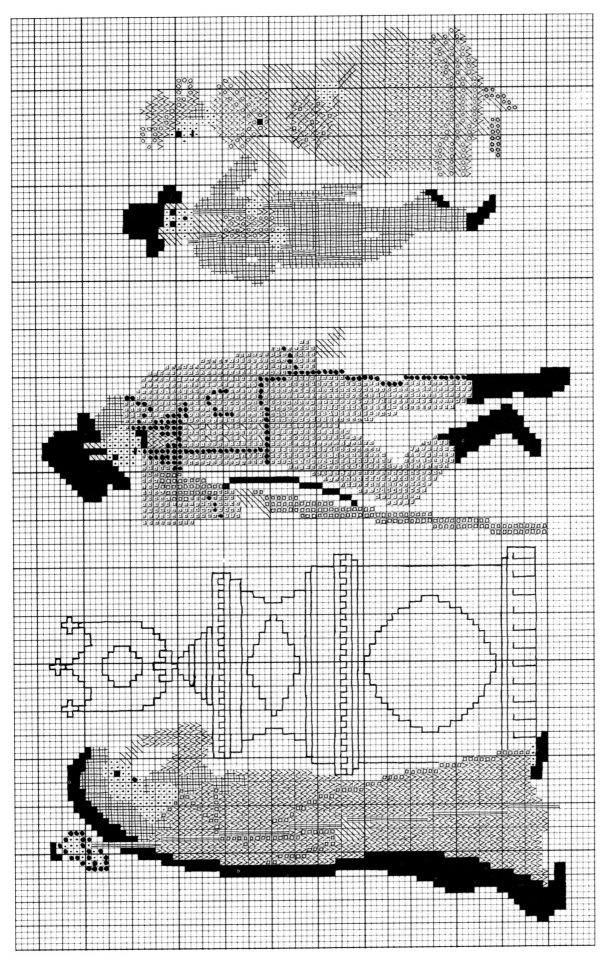

XVIII

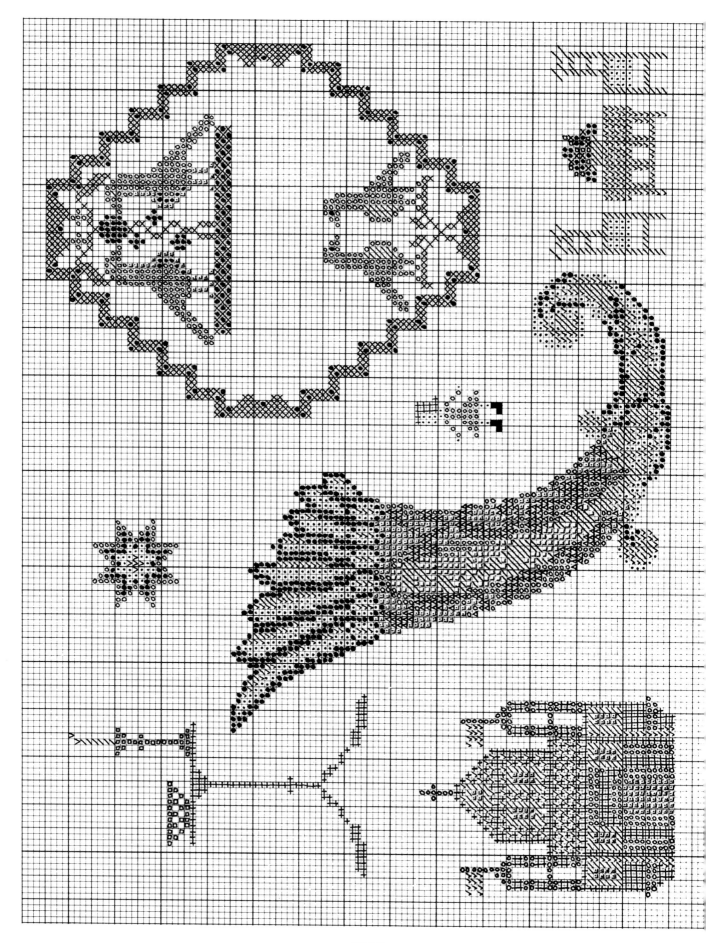

XIX

4

FOUR SAMPLERS
TO MAKE

Although the four samplers that follow may seem from the finished and framed products to be intricate and involved, none need be an "endless" project. The Pennsylvania-German sampler, stitched only in the evenings after the children were in bed and the house quiet, took only four weeks to complete. The other three samplers, also stitched by busy housewives and mothers, were each finished and mounted in the span of three months.

If you expect to carry your needlework around with you, you may wish to xerox the chart from which you are working. You can also enlarge the chart by having it photostated for a very nominal fee. Look in the classified section of your local phone book for places near you that do photostating. Be sure to ask for a positive (black on white).

Depending on the materials you choose to work with, your sampler could cost less than five dollars or more than twenty dollars to stitch. Because you have the freedom to choose your own materials, you can stay well within your budget and still have a lovely sampler.

✖

THE PENNSYLVANIA-GERMAN SAMPLER

✖

The Pennsylvania-German sampler, here adapted for modern embroiderers, was originally worked on linen in 1826 by Susana Landis, using silk and cotton entirely in cross stitch. She used black, red, green, blue, and white and edged the sampler with black ribbon drawn up into a scalloped edge. We used the same clear colors except for the substitution of pale yellow for the original white, which did not show enough contrast on our material. Our sampler has no border of any kind, but if you wish you can approximate the ribbon border by working satin stitches in a scallop pattern all the way around or by sewing black silk ribbon to the fabric as in the original (fig. 11). If you work a border, you will have to calculate the new overall dimensions of the sampler before you buy your fabric.

Our adaptation is 207 cross stitches wide by 216 cross stitches high. To find out how large a piece of fabric to buy and how big the finished sampler will be consult the chart below. If you are adding a border, adjust the measurements accordingly. The measurements are rounded to the nearest inch or half inch.

Fabric Threads per Inch	18	20	22	24	26	28	30	32
Cross Stitches to the Inch	9	10	11	12	13	14	15	16
Measurements of Worked Area in Inches	23 x 24	20½ x 21½	19 x 19½	17 x 18	16 x 16½	14½ x 15	14 x 14½	13 x 13½

Plan on having at least 6″ more fabric in each dimension. For instance, on the 24-mesh linen fabric that our adaptation is worked on, the worked measurements are 17″ x 18″. Therefore, cut your fabric to measure no less than 23″ x 24″. This extra fabric allows for a small hem to prevent the edges from fraying while you work, for 1½″ of unworked fabric inside the frame, and for the rest to be tacked on the back of the mounting board.

All of the following directions are based on our worked adaptation. If you are using different fabric and threads, experiment in a corner or on a sample scrap to find the correct thickness of thread to achieve the same relative effects, but follow the same general directions.

First put in a narrow hem all around by either hand rolling, binding with tape, or using the zig-zag stitch on your sewing machine. Begin work by folding your fabric in half lengthwise and marking a spot on the fold 3″ from the edge. This is the center top. Begin stitching there, working the large carnation between the two birds. When this motif is finished, you will find that the use of temporary guideline stitching will help in the placement of the remainder of the motifs. Put a row of guideline stitching down the center front. (See page 79 for instructions on guideline stitching.)

Now work the large rectangle which will hold your signature. Put 2 more rows of guideline stitching straight down on either side of the rectangle, and proceed with the remainder of the motifs, counting over from one motif to place the next. Most are placed close enough to each other so that this will not be too difficult.

Lynda Pullen, who worked our adaptation, placed her husband's initials in the large heart and those of her two children at the top on either side. Space is available for more initials if needed. They can be placed toward the outer edge of fabric beyond the eight-pointed stars, on either side of the top carnation, near the flower itself, and down the stem toward the roots. You can even move some of the charted motifs around to make more room for initials. In addition to an inscription above the motifs, the original sampler has ten sets of initials scattered throughout.

Work your signature last. (Consult page 54 for instructions on how to chart your name, place, and date on graph paper.)

Chart Symbol	Color Description	D.M.C. Pearl Cotton #8
●	red	321
X	green	701
V	yellow	745
O	blue	798
■	black	310

THE ADAM AND EVE FAMILY-RECORD SAMPLER

You will not find a sampler like this one in any book or collection of samplers. It was designed from single elements taken from many different sources, no two motifs (excluding Adam and Eve) taken from the same source. It is a perfect example of the lovely results that can be achieved by combining diverse traditional motifs to form a totally new sampler.

If you want to work this sampler, and the names you plan to include are as many and approximately as long as the Carkhuffs', then you do not have much paperwork before you start stitching. Consult page 54 for instructions on how to chart your own names and proceed with the stitching.

If, on the other hand, your names are much longer, or you have more than three children's names to include, you will have some rearranging to do. First chart all the names and dates on graph paper. If you have four children's names all you have to do is omit the bows on top of the swags, move everything up to fill that space, and stitch. When the lettering is completed, you will have to drop the red-checkerboard horizontal border a few stitches, but that is all the changing needed.

To add still more room, the blue satin-stitch border and the red-checkerboard border can be moved closer to the outer flower border, but be sure to do it on all four sides to preserve the symmetry. This change requires the addition of more satin-stitch grass in the width and length.

To add even more names, consider working all cross stitches over a single thread, as was done in many historic samplers. For this your working thread will have to be much finer than for the rest of the sampler. No changes in the overall design will be necessary if this method is used.

If you have two children's names, just add one blank row between each line of lettering and the given space will be filled neatly and evenly.

For a truly personal family record, consider omitting Adam and Eve entirely and inserting instead a representation of your own home.

Our sampler is 272 cross-stitches wide by 337 cross-stitches high. To find out how large a piece of fabric to buy and how big the finished sampler will be, consult the table below. The measurements are rounded to the nearest inch or half-inch.

Fabric Threads per Inch	18	20	22	24	26	28	30	32
Cross Stitches to the Inch	9	10	11	12	13	14	15	16
Measurements of Worked Area in Inches	30 x 37	27 x 33½	24½ x 30½	22½ x 28	21 x 26	19 x 24	18 x 22	17 x 21

Plan on having at least 6″ more fabric in each dimension. For example, if you plan on using the 20-thread-count linen which Mary Ann Carkhuff used, the worked measurements are 27″ x 33½″. Therefore, cut your fabric to measure no less than 33″ x 39½″. This extra fabric allows for a small hem to prevent edges from fraying while you work, for 1½″ of unworked fabric inside the frame, and for the rest to be tacked on the back of the mounting board.

The following directions are based on our worked adaptation. If you are using different fabric and threads, experiment in a corner or on a sample scrap to find the correct thickness of thread to achieve the same relative effects, but follow the same general directions. The sampler is worked in D.M.C. Pearl Cotton, size 8 for all cross stitch, size 5 for the satin stitch.

First put in a narrow hem all around by either hand rolling, binding with tape, or using the zig-zag stitch on your sewing machine. Begin work by folding your fabric in half lengthwise and marking a spot on the fold 3″ from the top. This is the center top and is where you will start stitching. The center of the chart is in the middle stitch of the fifth rose of the outer border. From this point, work the undulating green line of the border all the way around. After stitching 1 repeat of the border on each of the four sides, putting in 2 rows of guideline stitching will help relieve the endless counting and recounting of diagonal lines of stitches. Put 1 line along each straight area of stitching. (See page 79 for instructions on guideline stitching.) If you have counted correctly, when you are done you should have about 3″ to the edge of your fabric on all four sides.

Leave the rest of the border until last, since handling in working the interior elements of the sampler tends to rough up the stitches on the outer edges. If you wish to see how the colors and design of the border look, work just one repeat.

Skip the blue satin-stitch border (satin stitch gets mussed up even faster than cross stitch) and count over to the red-checkerboard border which you will do next.

Pl. VII.   *Pennsylvania-German sampler.*

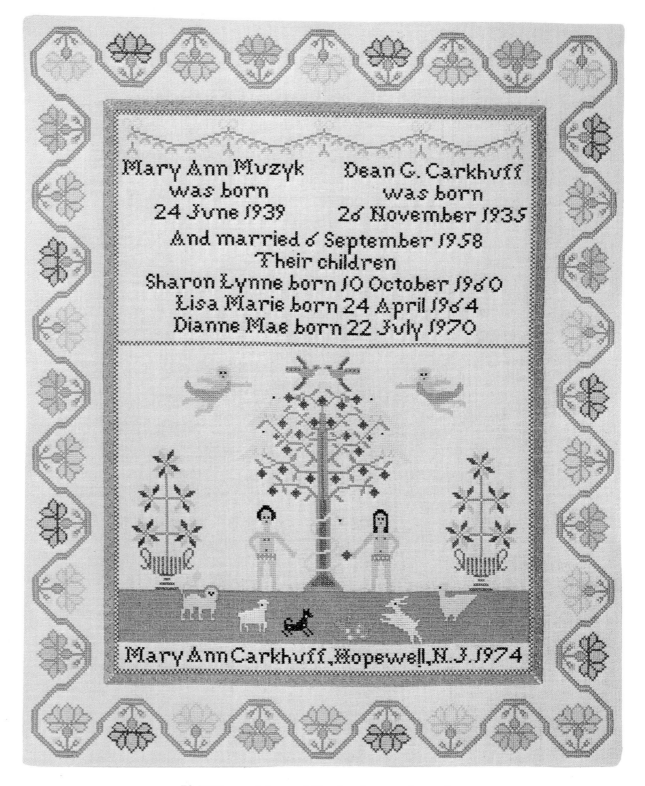

Pl. VIII.   *Adam and Eve family-record sampler.*

Pl. IX.   *Schoolhouse sampler.*

Pl. X.   *Alphabet sampler.*

A row of guideline stitching straight down the center will help from here on. Work the swag and flower motif, then all your lettering. It is easier to work each line of lettering from the center out to each side. Put in the horizontal checkerboard border.

Next work the flying birds, the tree and snake, Adam and Eve, the animals, and the flower urns, in that order. Guideline stitching going up from the urn and over from the flying birds will help place the cherubs correctly.

Now fill in the flowers in the outer border. Departing from tradition, stitch your signature now, and then work the large areas of satin stitch in the grass and the blue border. Working these areas last will spare them from being roughed up too much in handling.

The following thread directions refer to size 8 D.M.C. Pearl Cotton. Those numbers marked with an asterisk indicate that the same color is also used in size 5.

Symbol	Color Description	D.M.C. Pearl Cotton
●	red	891
·	pink	353
‖	dark brown	434
+	brown	436
X	green	911*
—	light green	590
V	yellow	744
O	blue	334*
■	black	310

Dean C. Carkhuff
was born
26 November 1935

Mary Ann Muzyk
was born
24 June 1939

And married 6 September 1958

Their children

Sharon Lynne born 10 October 1960
Lisa Marie born 24 April 1964
Dianne Mae born 22 July 1970

The original on which this sampler is based was worked by Mary Fowser, probably in Quinton (Salem County), New Jersey, circa 1835. Possibly a representation of the Quinton School, it was worked in wool on 20-mesh canvas. The dimensions inside the frame are 20½″ high by 21¼″ wide.

Most of Mary Fowser's sampler seems to have been done from patterns laid out by her teacher or copied from a book or from other samplers, but the three charming flower bushes behind the fences are very free and irregular and were probably designs of her own fancy, possibly evolving as she stitched. She had the same problem most young sampler makers had, that of turning the corners of her border neatly. She did not even try, but ran them in straight lines, stopping one only where it ran into the next.

Our modern adaptation has neatly-cornered borders. This necessitated enlarging the design, especially in the width.

The measurements of the sampler along the outer edges of the border are 231 cross-stitches high by 279 cross-stitches wide. To find out how large a piece of fabric to buy and how big the finished sampler will be, consult the table below. The measurements are rounded to the nearest inch or half-inch.

Fabric Threads per Inch	18	20	22	24	26	28	30	32
Cross Stitches to the Inch	9	10	11	12	13	14	15	16
Measurements of Worked Area in Inches	25½ x 31	23 x 28	21 x 25	19 x 23	18 x 21½	16½ x 20	15 x 18½	14 x 17

Plan on having at least 6″ more fabric in each dimension. For instance, on the 18-mesh linen fabric that our adaptation is worked on, the worked measurements are 25½″ x 31″. Therefore, cut your fabric to measure no less than 31½″ x 37″. This extra fabric allows for a small hem to prevent the edges from fraying while you work, for 1½″ of unworked fabric inside the frame, and for the rest to be tacked on the back of the mounting board.

All of the following directions are based on our worked adaptation. If you are using different fabric and threads, experiment in a corner or on a sample scrap to find the correct thickness of thread to achieve the same relative effects, but follow the same general directions.

All cross stitch is done with 2 strands of Persian wool, except for the top line of each chimney, which is done with 3 strands. Eyelet and fly stitches are done with 2 strands, tent and satin stitch with 3 strands.

First put in a narrow hem all around by either hand rolling, binding with tape, or using the zig-zag stitch on your sewing machine. Begin work by folding your fabric in half lengthwise and marking a spot on the fold 3″ from the edge. This is the center top and is where you will start stitching. The center top of the chart is between the eleventh and twelfth large strawberries on the border. From this point work the undulating green line of the border all the way around. If you have counted correctly, when you are done you should have about 3″ to the edge of your fabric on all four sides. Leave the rest of the border until last, since handling in working the interior elements tends to rough up the stitches on the outer edges. If you wish to see how the colors and design of the border look, work just one repeat.

Starting in the middle and working to the left, then to the right, work the first line of the alphabet in cross stitch. You will find this and all of the following steps easier if you first put in a row of guideline stitching from border to border, top to bottom, along the center thread or stitch. Guideline stitching can also be done at the top and bottom of an undulating line in a border so that you are not endlessly counting and recounting stitches on a diagonal line. (See page 79 for instructions on guideline stitching.) After working the first alphabet line, work the first small border in eyelet stitch, the second alphabet in cross stitch, and then the second border in satin stitch.

Starting at the center chimney, outline the schoolhouse in tent stitch, remembering that the top line of each chimney is done in cross stitch using 3 strands. Then work the windows and doors in tent stitch and the white lines in cross stitch. Work the window sills and foundation in satin stitch. Do the grey tin roof and steps in cross stitch, then finish filling in the schoolhouse in tent stitch.

When the schoolhouse and steps are done, work the side fences and gates, the front fence and gates, then the trees and bushes in cross stitch and fly stitch. Then do the dogs, birds, and the remainder of the border, all in cross stitch.

To complete your sampler stitch your signature. (Consult page 54 for instructions on how to chart your own name, place, and date on graph paper.)

Chart Symbol	Color Description	Paternayan Yarn
●	red	242
·	middle red	843
√	pink	853
X	green	527
—	middle green	590
△	grey	162
/	white	005
O	light blue	396
V	yellow	442

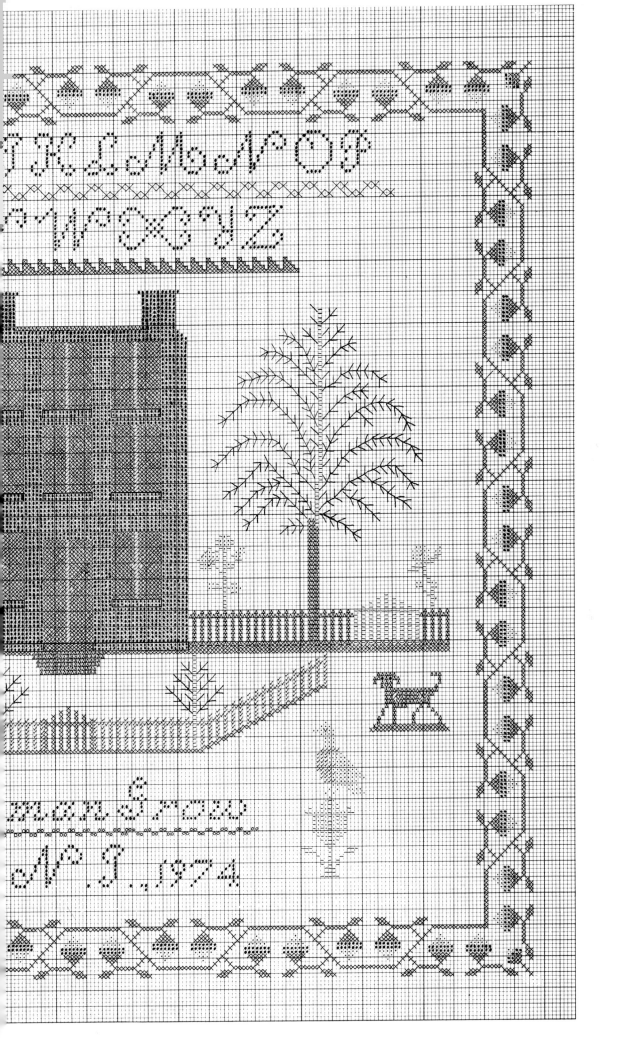

The alphabet sampler is adapted from the sampler which can be seen in plate I. The original was done in Philadelphia in 1737 by Elizabeth Hudson, who worked the sampler on linen in cross and satin stitches of green, red, brown, blue, yellow, white, cream, and tan silk. We have eliminated some of her cross borders, changed others, and inserted our alphabets and signature where she put verses. We have also used a pure white fabric intead of the original tan.

Our adaptation is 207 cross-stitches wide by 325 cross-stitches high. To find out how large a piece of fabric to buy and how big the finished sampler will be, consult the table below. The measurements are rounded to the nearest inch or half-inch.

Fabric Threads Per Inch	18	20	22	24	26	28	30	32
Cross Stitches to the Inch	9	10	11	12	13	14	15	16
Measurements of Worked Area in Inches	23 x 26	20½ x 32½	19 x 29½	17 x 27	16 x 25	15 x 23	14 x 21	13 x 20

Plan on having at least 6″ more fabric in each dimension. For example, if you plan on using the 22-thread-count cotton Hardanger cloth which Gedske Szepsy used, the worked measurements are 19″ x 29½″. Therefore, cut your fabric to measure no less than 25″ x 35½″. This extra fabric allows for a small hem to prevent the edges from fraying while you work, for 1½″ of unworked fabric inside the frame, and for the rest to be tacked on the back of the mounting board.

All of the following directions are based on our worked adaptation. If you are using different fabric and threads, experiment in a corner or on a sample scrap to find the correct thickness of thread to achieve the same relative effects, but follow the same general directions.

First put in a narrow hem all around by either hand rolling, binding with tape, or using the zig-zag stitch on your sewing machine. Begin work by folding your fabric in half lengthwise and marking a spot on the fold 3″ from the edge. This is the center top and is where you will start stitching. The center top of the chart is in the middle stitch of the fourth carnation of the outer border. From this point work the undulating green line of the border all the way around. After stitching 1 repeat of the border on each of the four sides, putting in 2 rows of guideline stitching will help relieve the endless counting and recounting of diagonal lines of stitches. Put one line along each straight area of stitching. (See page 79 for instructions on guideline stitching.) Notice that on this sampler the number of stitches in the center at both the top and bottom is different from all the other repeats. If you have counted correctly, when you are done you should have about 3″ to the edge of your fabric on all four sides. Leave the rest of the border until last, since handling in working the interior elements tends to rough up the stitches on the outer edges. If you wish to see how the colors and design of the border look, work just one repeat.

Now work the single-line pale-pink border all the way around. When this is done, you will find all of the folowing steps easier if you first put in a row of guideline stitching from border to border, top to bottom, along the center thread or stitch.

Work the first satin-stitch cross-border, then the cross-stitch alphabet, starting it in the center and stitching to either side. Then work the next satin-stitch cross-border. Continue in this manner all the way down, leaving the signature lines for last. Note that the strawberry in the second floral cross-border is done in vertical satin stitches and that the large rose in the fourth cross-border is filled in with satin stitches done vertically in the top two and bottom two petals, horizontally in the two petals on either side.

To complete your sampler, work the carnations in the encircling border and then stitch your signature. (Consult page 54 for instructions on how to chart your own name, place, and date on graph paper.)

All the designs in this book can be modified to suit your fancy by changing colors, size, stitches and even motifs. For instance, a second alphabet sampler can be made using the same chart as the sampler presented here, but with some changes. All the blues are deleted and replaced by a fourth green. The reds are changed to a family of geranium shades, and the brown made darker. The sampler is done on a 24-thread-count natural-colored linen and its dimensions are smaller. When the interior of the sampler is completed and all that remains is to fill in the carnations in the outer border, you may, if you wish, prefer to change the border itself. For example, a tulip from another border may be adapted to fill the same space as the carnation with leaves made to fit along the undulating green line, transforming the whole into a far more complex and important border. By these few changes the two alphabet samplers can look quite different, but equally lovely, when placed side by side. Borders numbered 30 and 31 on Chart VI are the two that can be used for these samplers.

Symbol	Color Description	D.M.C. Pearl Cotton #8
●	red	891
·	medium red	893
√	pink	819
+	brown	436
X	green	909
—	medium green	911
Z	light green	703
V	yellow	745
⌊·	blue	519
O	dark blue	517

✖ *Four Samplers To Make* ✖

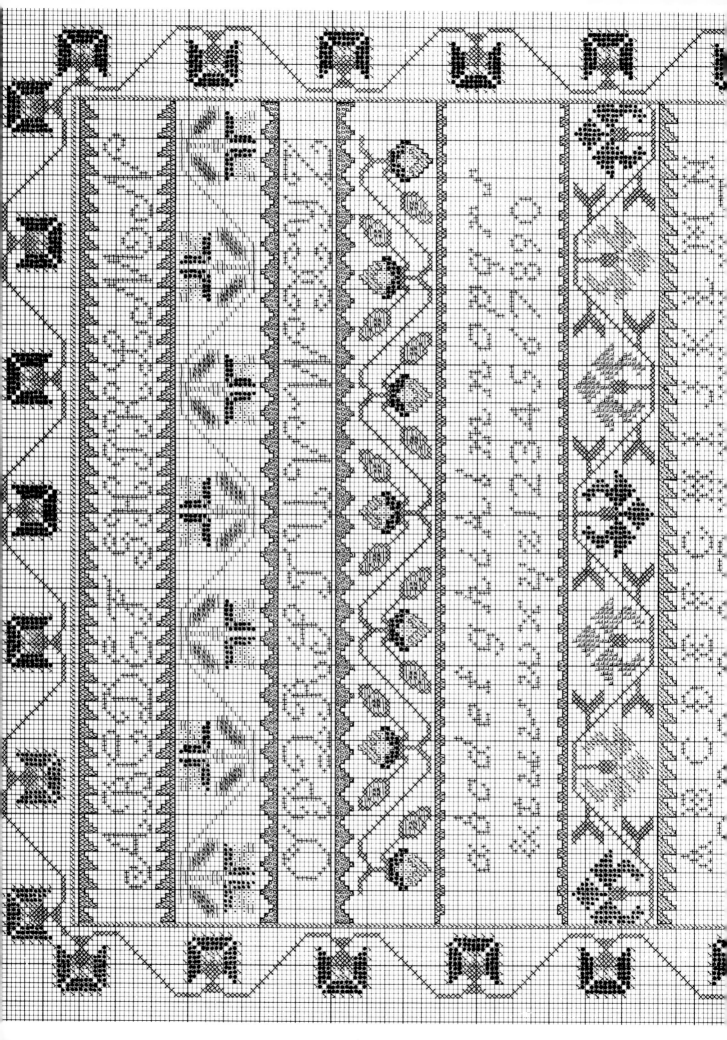

APPENDICES

COLLECTIONS OF HISTORICAL AMERICAN SAMPLERS

Collections of antique samplers can be seen in many museum and historical society collections. Only a very few are listed here. Most local historical societies, at least in the eastern United States, have interesting collections of samplers. These are informative places to view examples because the samplers often come with a reliable history of local origin and are therefore a good indication of the type of work done in a particular area. Often, also, the samplers will be displayed in such a way that they can be seen close-up. The following list indicates a few of the larger institutions which have important or extensive collections of American needlework.

New England:

Shelburne Museum, Inc.
US Route 7
Shelburne, Vermont 05482

The Essex Institute
132 Essex Street
Salem, Massachusetts 01970

The Boston Museum of Fine Arts
Huntington Avenue
Boston, Massachusetts 02115

Middle States:

The Jewish Museum
1109 Fifth Avenue
New York, New York 10028

The New-York Historical Society
170 Central Park West
New York, New York 10024

Philadelphia Museum of Art
26th Street and Benjamin Franklin Parkway
Philadelphia, Pennsylvania 19101

DAR Museum
Memorial Continental Hall
1776 D. Street, N. W.
Washington, D. C. 20006

The Midwest:

The Art Institute of Chicago
Michigan Avenue at Adams Street
Chicago, Illinois 60603

The South:

Valentine Museum
1015 E. Clay Street
Richmond, Virginia 23219

Old Salem, Inc.
Drawer F, Salem Station
Winston-Salem, North Carolina 27108

In addition, selections from the Philadelphia Museum of Art's outstanding Whitman Sampler Collection are available as a travelling exhibit. Information can be obtained from the museum's Costume and Textile Department.

The DAR Museum in Washington has prepared a slide lecture, illustrating forty American samplers and needlework pictures from their collection, with accompanying text. The program can be rented for a nominal fee. Information can be obtained from the museum.

✖ *Appendices* ✖

SUPPLIERS OF MATERIALS

Supplies for samplers and other forms of counted-thread embroidery can be purchased at many needlework shops around the country. If you are not sure of the location of such shops in your area, check the yellow pages of your local telephone directory under "Art Needlework." The needlework departments of many large department stores are also good sources for materials.

If you cannot find what you need locally, here is a partial list of shops that sell by mail. Those that provide catalogs are marked with an asterisk:

Northeast
The Crafts Center
Quaker Road
Nantucket, Mass. 02554

*Boutique Margot
26 West 54th Street
New York, N. Y. 10019

Crafty Women
Colts Town Shoppes
Highway 34
Colts Neck, N. J. 08750

Janet's
Highway 35
Sea Girt, N. J. 08750

*Nordicraft
356 Nassau Street
Princeton, N. J. 08540

South
Hook, Braid, 'n Needle
Crafts Center
3742 Howard Avenue
Kensington, Md. 20795

The Elegant Needle
5430 MacArthur Blvd., N. W.
Washington, D. C. 20016

Yarns Etcetera
215 King Street
Alexandria, Va. 22314

Laura Weaver Needlework
Hotel Patrick Henry
617 South Jefferson Street
Roanoke, Va. 24011

Ruth Leary's
382 North Elm Street
Greensboro, N. C. 27401

The Snail's Pace
548 East Paces Ferry Road, N. E.
Atlanta, Ga. 30305

Yarn and Design Studio
4061 Ponce de Leon Boulevard
Coral Gables, Fla. 33134

Deux Amis
The Establishment
3708 Crawford
Austin, Tex. 78731

Virginia Maxwell
Custom Needlework Studio
3404 Kirby Drive
Houston, Tex. 77006

*Merribee Company
Box 9680
Fort Worth, Tex. 76107

Midwest
The Sampler
1011 South Washington
Royal Oak, Mich. 48067

*Lee Wards
1200 Saint Charles Street
Elgin, Ill. 60120

*Herrschners Needlecrafts
Hoover Road
Stevens Point, Wis. 54481

Stitch Niche
2866 Hennepin Avenue
Minneapolis, Minn. 55408

West
The Yarn Garden, Inc.
10956 North May Avenue
Oklahoma City, Ok. 73120

*The Needlecraft Shop
4501 Van Nuys Boulevard
Sherman Oaks, Calif. 91403

*Thumbelina Needlework Shop
1685 Copenhagen Drive
Solvang, Calif. 93463

Phalice's Thread Web
West 1301 14th Avenue
Spokane, Wash. 99204

SELECTED BIBLIOGRAPHY

history of needlework

Bolton, Ethel Stanwood and Coe, Eva Johnston. *American Samplers.* Boston, 1921. Reprint. Princeton, N.J.: The Pyne Press, 1973.

_____. "Five Contemporary Samplers." *Antiques* XIV (July, 1928), 52–54.

Caulfield, Sophia Frances Anne and Saward, Blanche C. *The Dictionary of Needlework.* London, 1882. Reprint. New York: Arno Press, n.d.

Garrett, Elizabeth Donagy. "American Samplers and Needlework Pictures in the DAR Museum." *Antiques* CV (February, 1974), 356–364.

Harbeson, Georgianna Brown. *American Needlework.* New York, 1938. Reprint. New York: Bonanza Books, n.d.

Horner, Mariánna Merritt. *The Story of Samplers.* Philadelphia: Philadelphia Museum of Art, 1971.

Huish, Marcus. *Samplers and Tapestry Embroideries.* 2d ed. London, 1913. Reprint. New York: Dover Publishing Co., 1970.

Keith, Elmer D. "Architectural Sidelights from Samplers." *Antiques* VLII (June, 1950), 437–438.

Ring, Betty. "Collecting American Samplers Today." *Antiques* CI (June, 1972), 1012–1018.

Schiffer, Margaret B. *Historical Needlework of Pennsylvania.* New York: Charles Scribner's Sons, 1968.

working embroidery

Christie, Mrs. Archibald. *Samplers and Stitches.* London, 1920. Reprint. Great Neck, N.Y.: Hearthside Press, 1971.

Davis, Mildred J. *The Art of Crewel Embroidery.* South Hackensack, N.J.: Spinnerin Yarn Co., Inc., 1962.

de Dillmont, Therese. *Encyclopedia of Needlework.* Paris: D. M. C. Library, n.d.

Dreesmann, Cécile. *Samplers for Today.* New York: Van Nostrand Reinhold Co., 1972.

Enthoven, Jacqueline. *The Stitches of Creative Embroidery.* New York: Rheinhold Publishing Corp., 1964.

Hanley, Hope. *Needlepoint.* New York: Charles Scribner's Sons, 1964.

Thomas, Mary. *Mary Thomas's Dictionary of Embroidery Stitches.* New York: Gramercy Pub. Co., 1935.

_____. *Mary Thomas's Embroidery Book.* New York: Gramercy Pub. Co., 1936.

Wilson, Erica. *Erica Wilson's Embroidery Book.* New York: Charles Scribner's Sons, 1973.

✖ *Appendices* ✖

when else
all fails

when
all else
fails =

$$33$$
$$\times 9$$
$$\overline{297}$$

$\times 200$

200×300

6×9